Oh The Moon

HARPER ⬤ PERENNIAL

NEW YORK • LONDON • TORONTO • SYDNEY • NEW DELHI • AUCKLAND

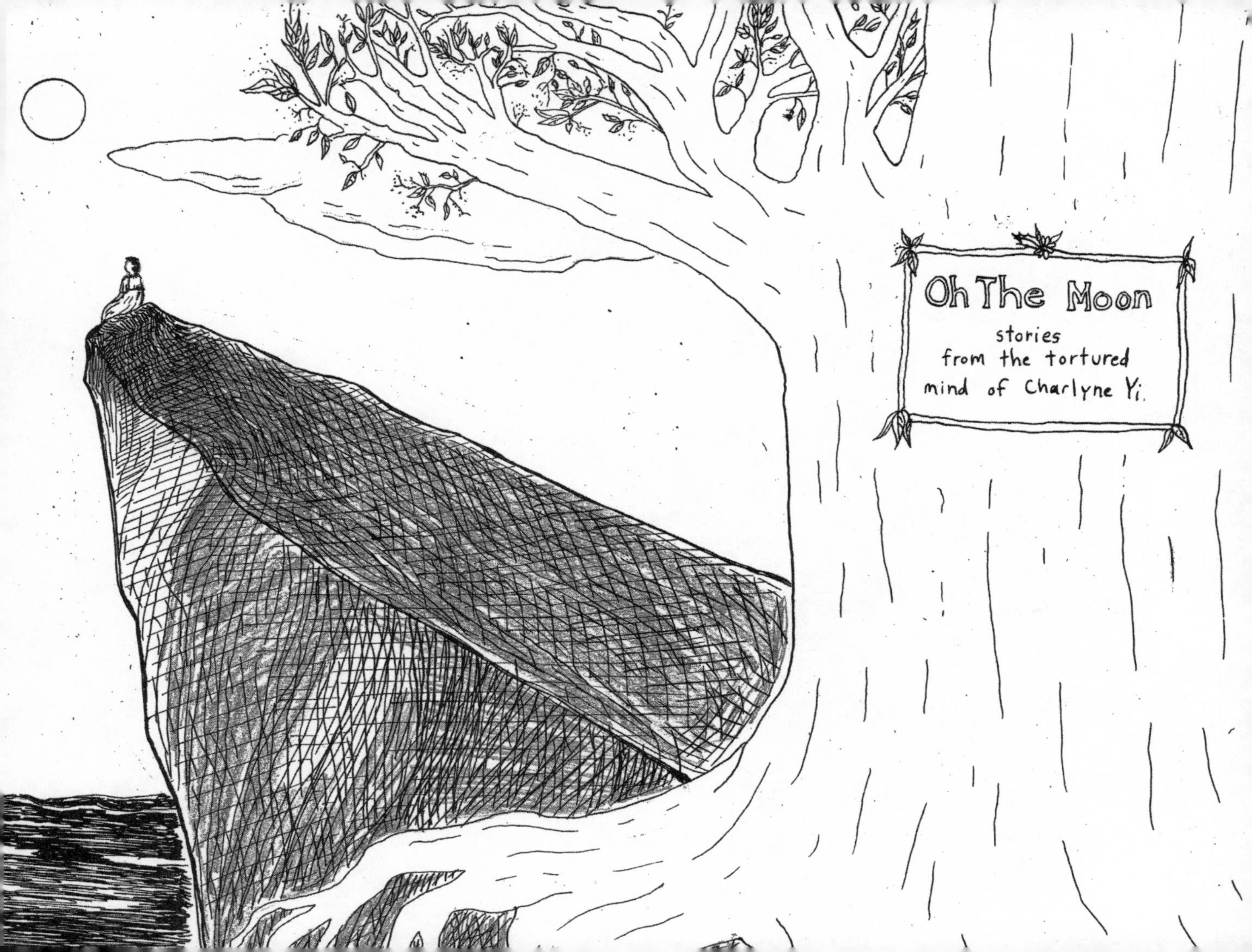
Oh The Moon
stories
from the tortured
mind of Charlyne Yi.

HARPER ● PERENNIAL

HarperCollins books may be purchased for educational, business, or sales promotional use. For information please e-mail the Special Markets Department at SPsales@harpercollins.com.

FIRST EDITION

Designed by Jamie Lynn Kerner

Library of Congress Cataloging-in-Publication Data has been applied for.

ISBN 978-0-06-236329-9 (pbk.)

15 16 17 18 19   OV/RRD   10 9 8 7 6 5 4 3 2 1

for you

CONTENTS

INTRODUCTION

Hi. My name is Charlyne. I am . . . an adult. I wasn't always an adult. I used to be a little kid. I didn't really have friends back then, even imaginary ones didn't want to hang out with me. I spent most of my time alone, daydreaming. With that I grew a really strong imagination. Super buff. But I lived mostly in my head and didn't know how to function in the real world until . . .

One day, I turned 18 and POOF I became an adult! I moved out and started to do comedy. I had to live in my car, but it wasn't safe to sleep there at night. So I stayed up at night like Batman and drank lots of coffee in diners . . . just like Batman. By day I slept at the park and became friends with homeless folks and regulars at bars. These people opened their hearts up to me, trying to teach me things that they had learned.

And it was the magic of us exchanging these bubbles of memories and stories that allowed us to connect, pass time, and laugh while we cried . . .

Like the strangers that opened up to me, I'd like to share something with you: I'd like to share with you my heart and the memories that changed my life.

Alright . . . deep breath. Here we go!

FORGIVE ME

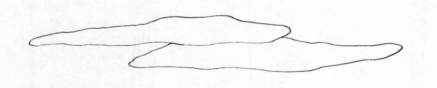

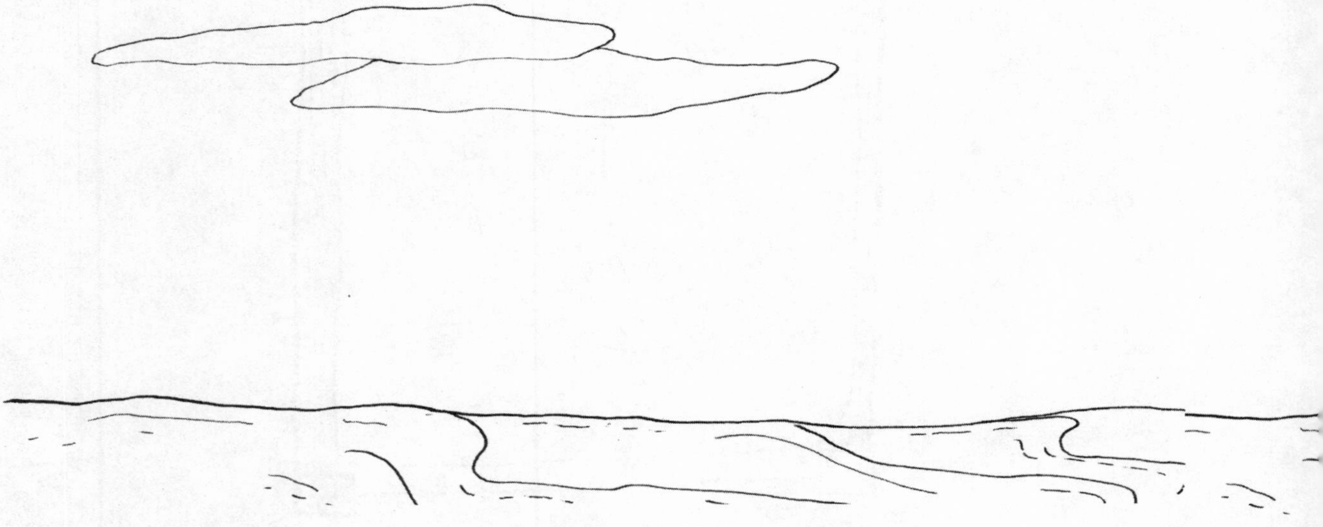

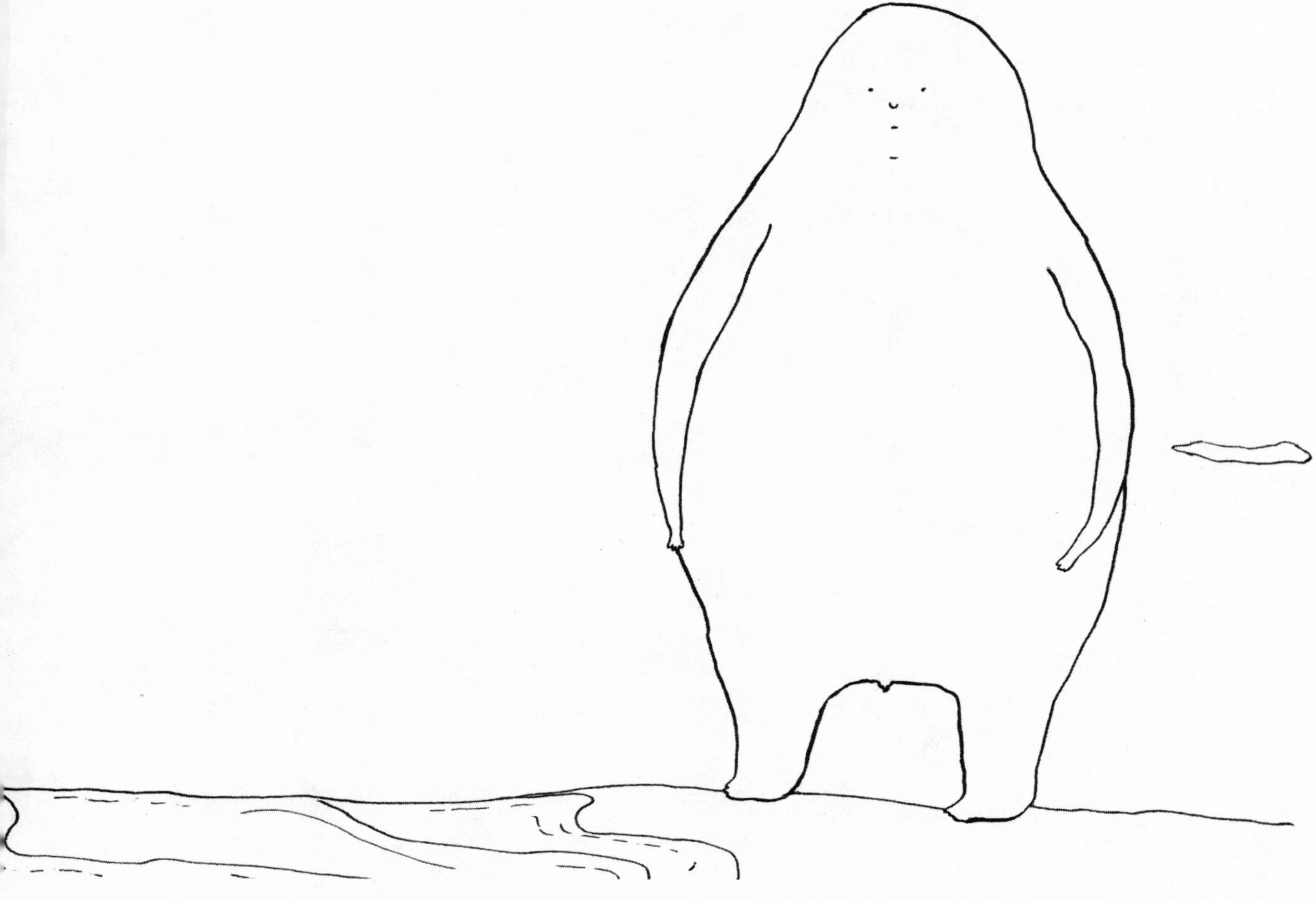

It was night. And a chimney puffed clouds of smoke,
giving company to the other clouds in the sky.

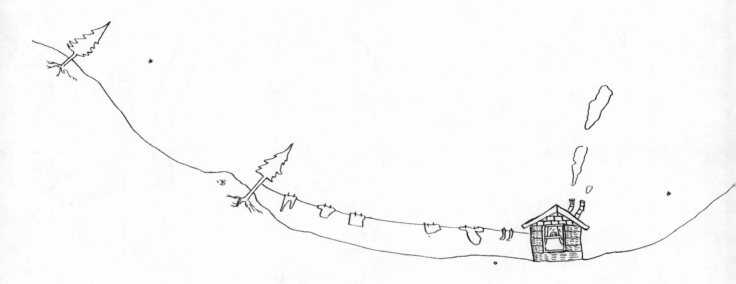

Something big was happening in a little house.

Old Ms. Jenkins was giving birth to a giant!

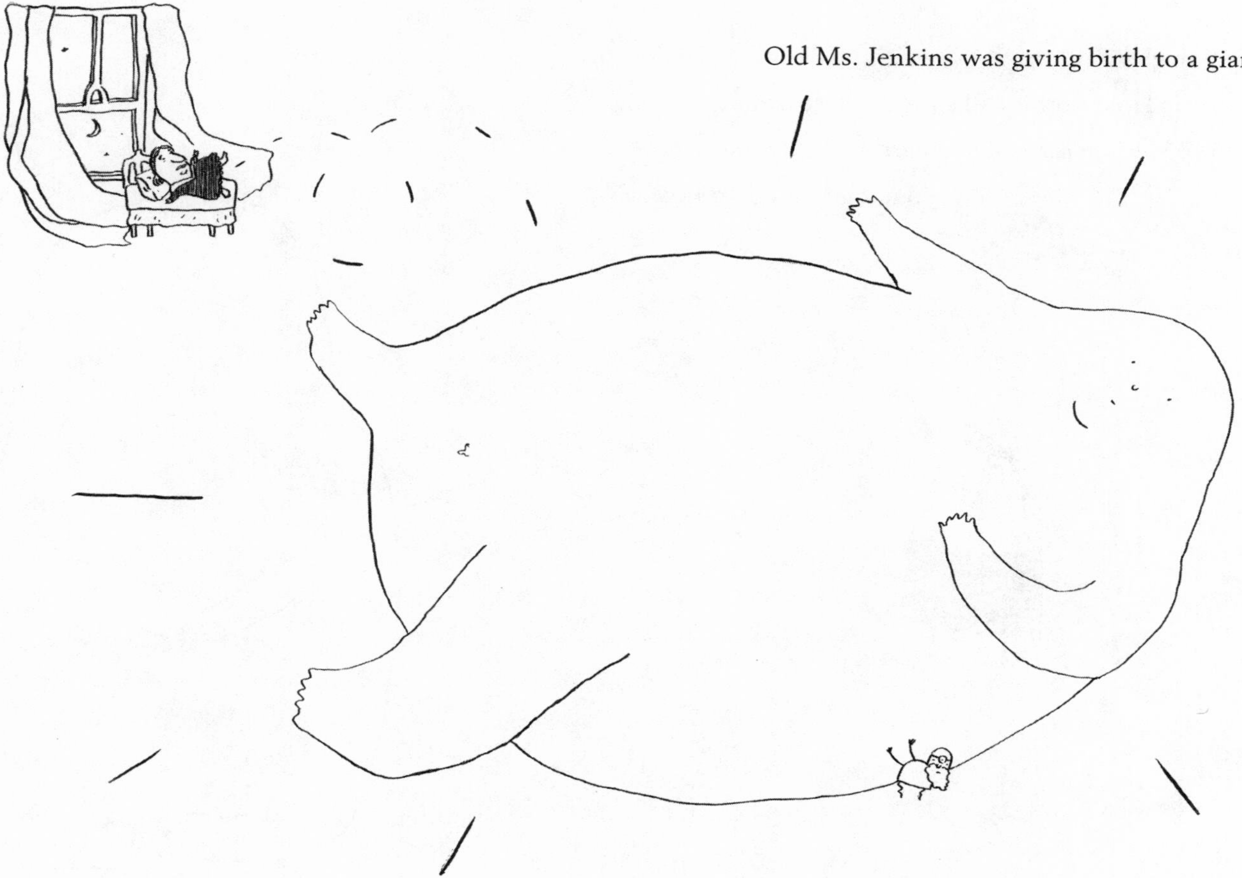

She thought,

"He looks nothing like me, his face is much too big.

Mine is small and narrow.

I definitely did not give birth to this baby."

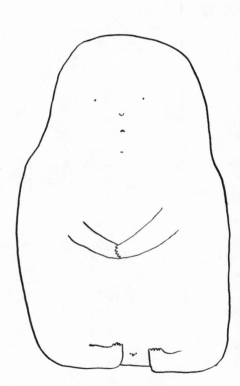

"I'm sorry but you're too big for me to love.
I don't have enough love in me to love you, for I am
small."

Fearful of what she had created, she banished her only son.

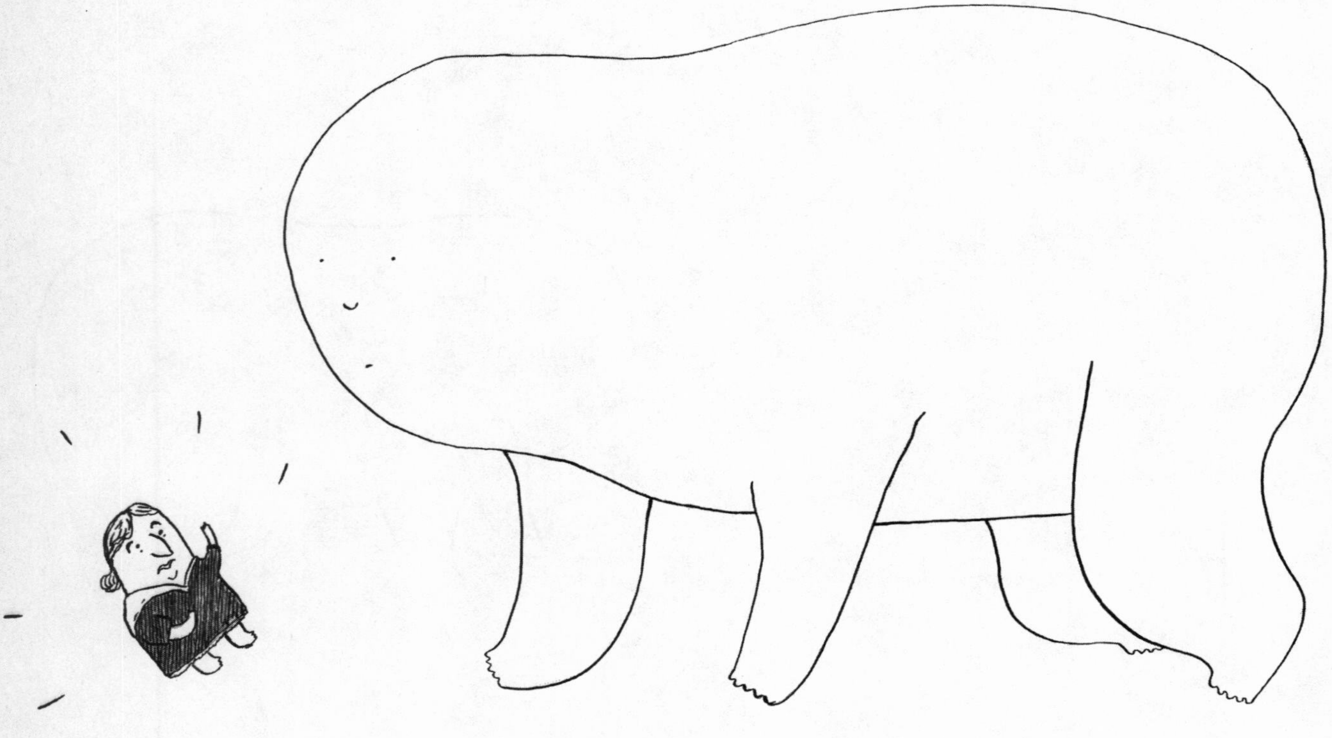

The infant couldn't make his mother love him.
So he had to learn how to walk on his own.

And so, he took his first steps
out and into the world . . .

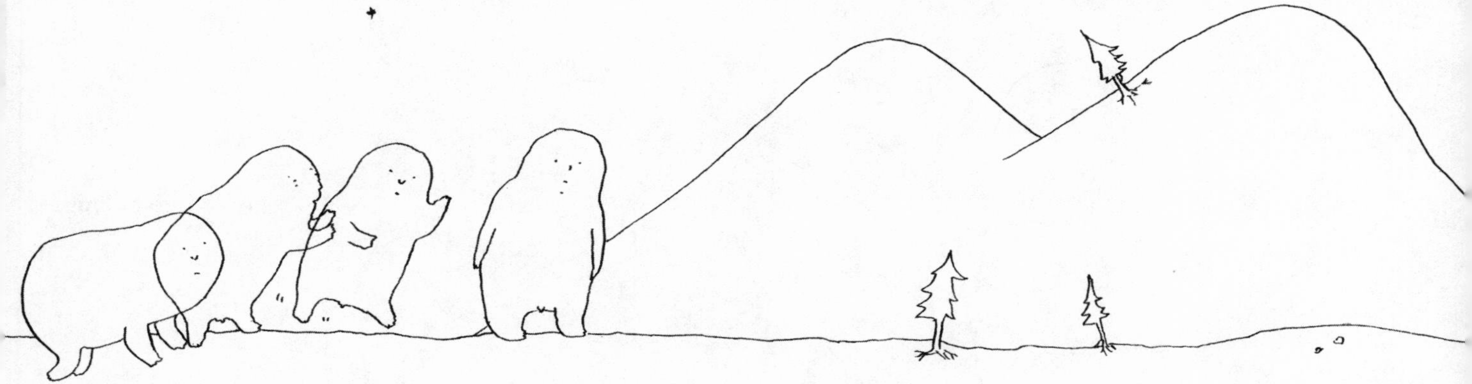

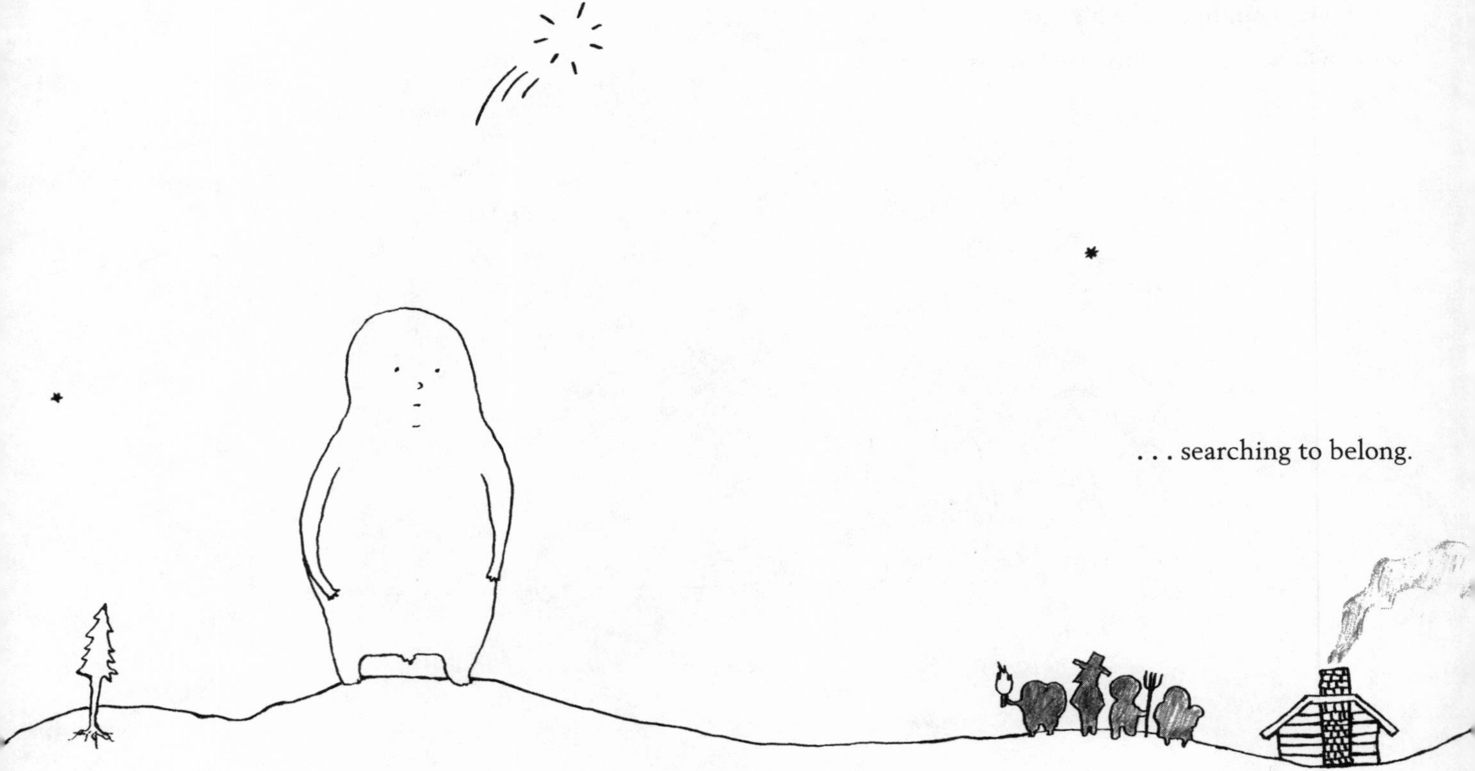

. . . searching to belong.

A villager moved closer and studied the visitor.

"Look at him, he's not like us!

"Well, actually, he's exactly like us BUT BIGGER!

"And that's just not normal . . . he's a monster," the angry man concluded.

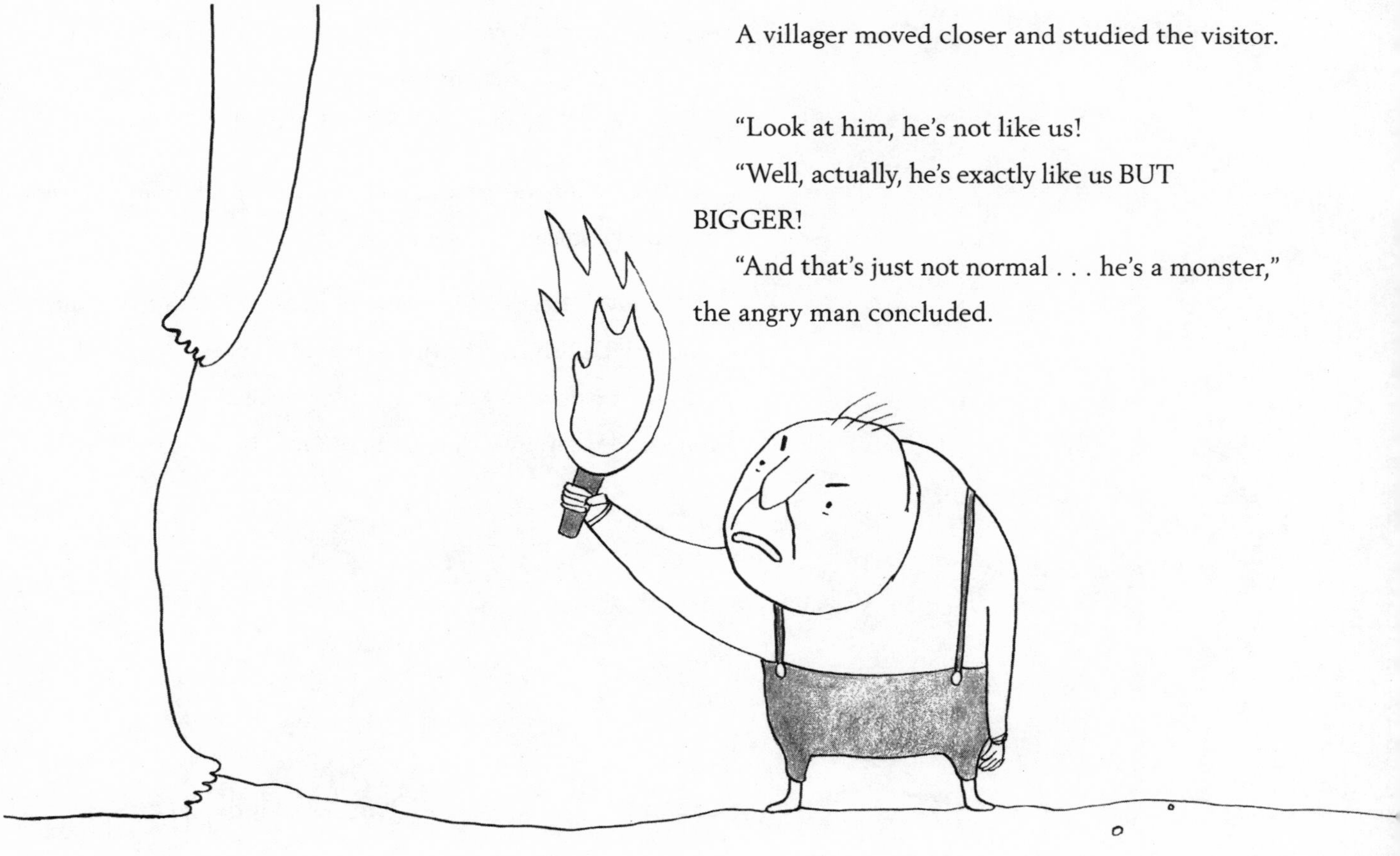

The angry villager introduced the town to him,

"Monster, this is our town . . .

Town, this is an unwelcome MONSTER!"

The infant was never taught how to speak so he couldn't explain he meant no harm.

Ready to destroy him they threw their fists into the air, when SUDDENLY, the tiniest boy of all time came to the rescue. He stood as tall as he could between them, because he too knew what it was like to be unloved because of his size.

WHO'S THE REAL MONSTER? LOOK AT YOU!

GET OUTTA THE WAY, KID!

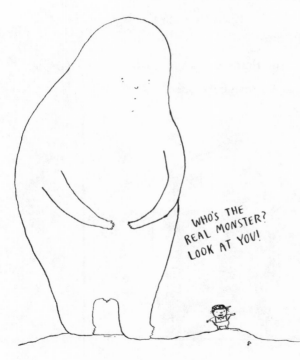

A cloudy memory stormed into the
tiny boy's head.

"Congratulations, I heard you had a baby,"
a neighbor greeted. "I would love to meet him."

"Of course," the excited father replied.

The father brought his tiny baby out, "Here he is,
isn't he beautiful?"

"Where is he?" the confused neighbor asked.

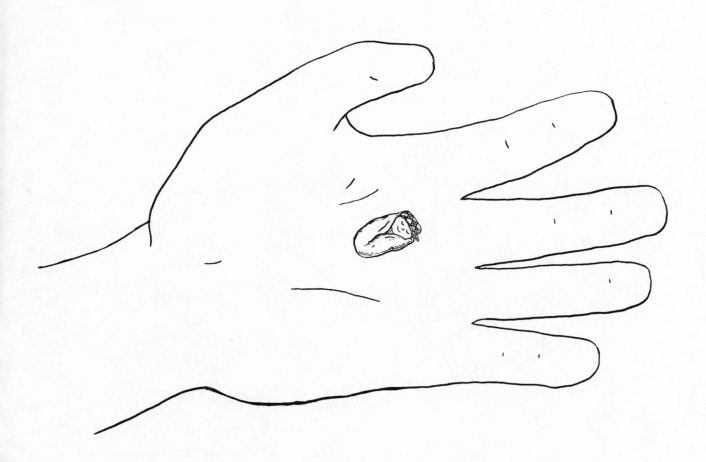

The neighbor laughed right in their faces,

"You have an ANT for a son?!"

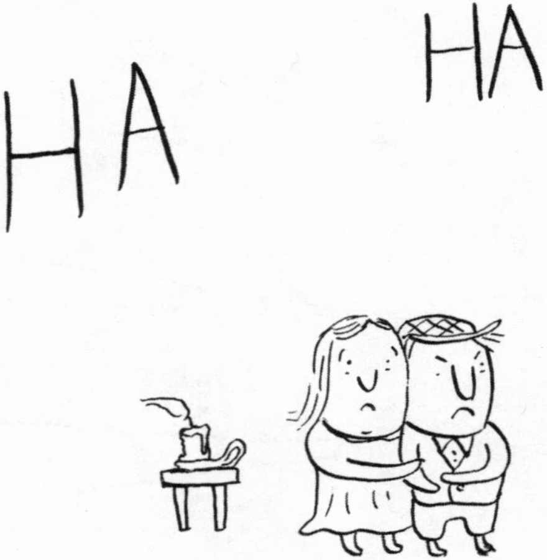
HA
HA

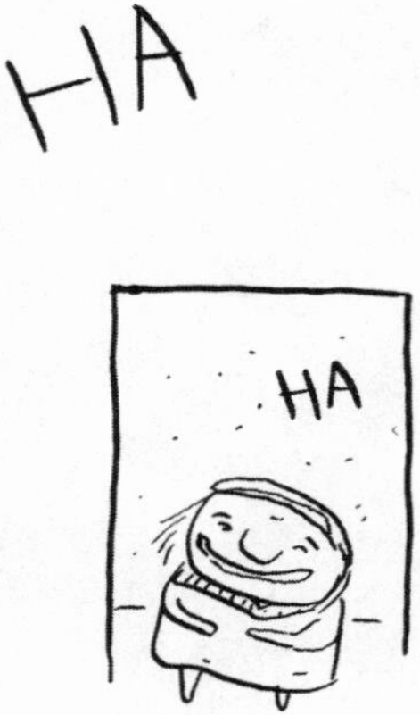
HA
HA

She went about her way, the parents hearing every "HA"

as she laughed all the way home.

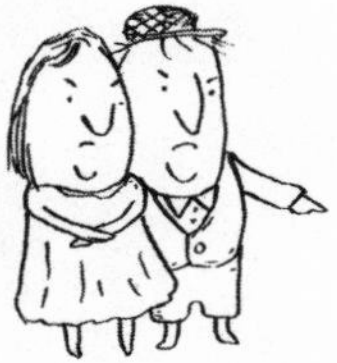

WHO COULD EVER LOVE SOMETHING SO SMALL

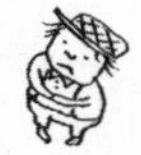

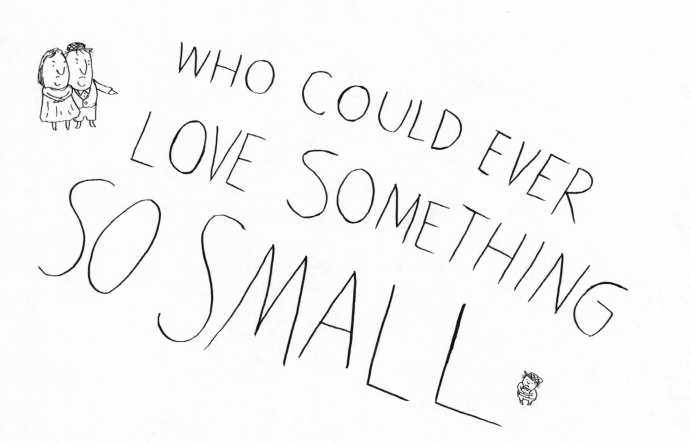

Now, this didn't exactly happen.
After all, this is a cloudy memory.
However, his parents were awfully
embarrassed of their tiny son, and he
was able to feel those big feelings.

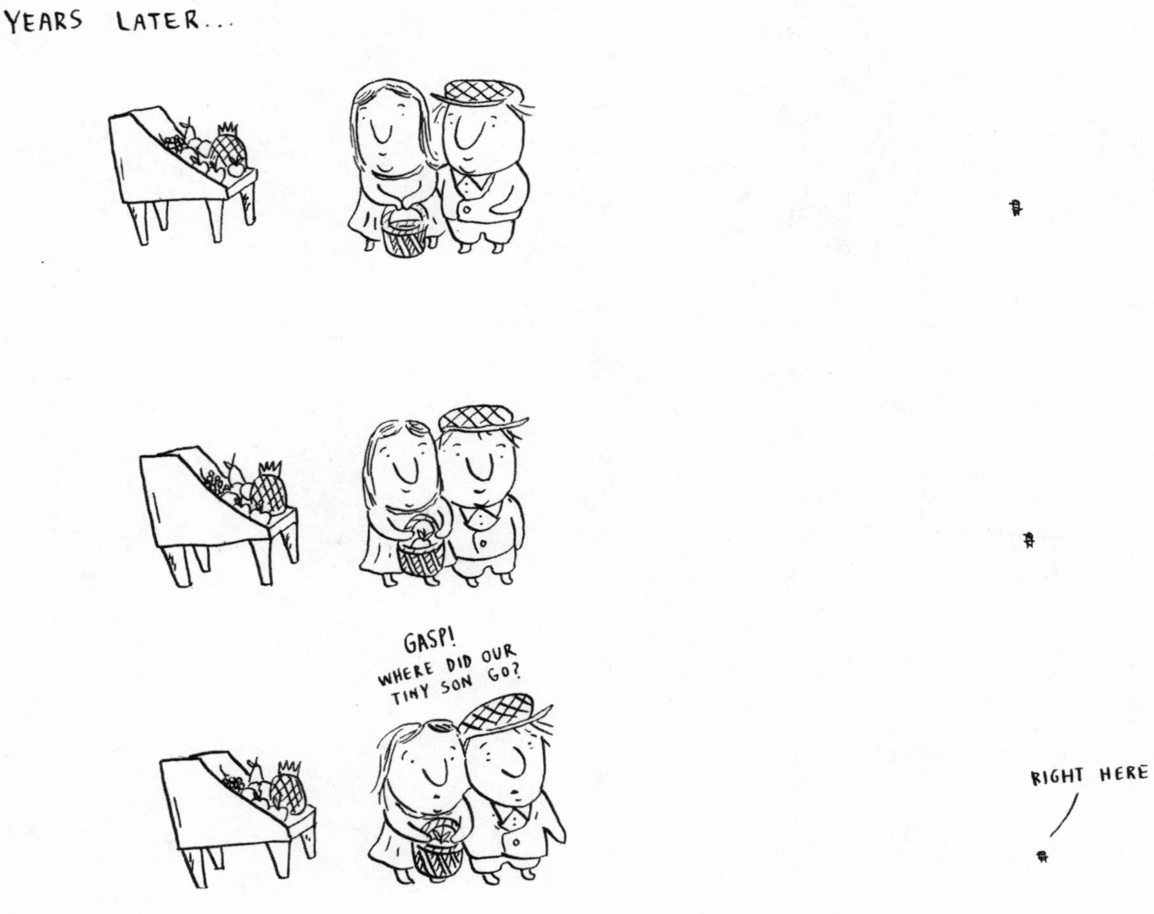
YEARS LATER...
GASP!
WHERE DID OUR TINY SON GO?
RIGHT HERE

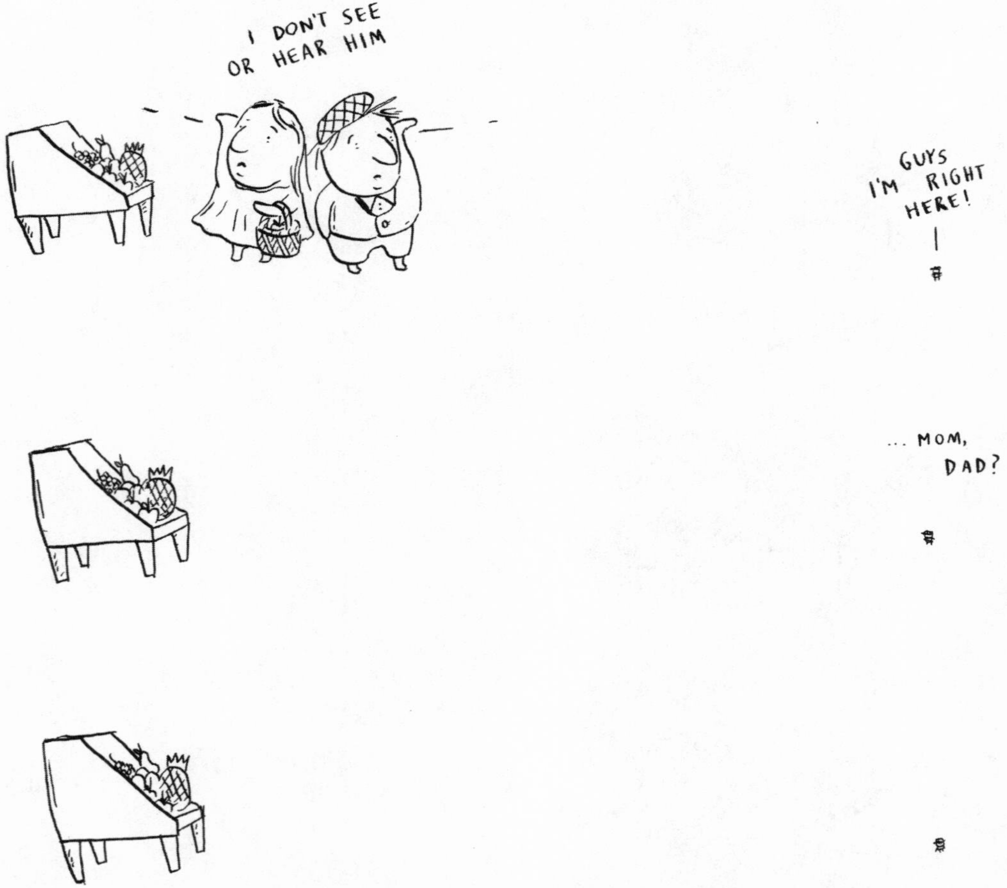
I DON'T SEE OR HEAR HIM
GUYS I'M RIGHT HERE!
... MOM, DAD?

"Never again," the tiny boy thought to himself.

"From hence on, I shall be heard."

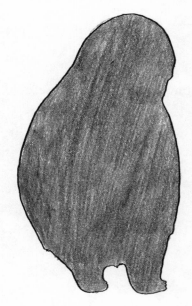

THIS MUST END!
I WILL NOT
STAND FOR
THIS!

20

The villagers were still angry.

And with a toss of a stone . . .

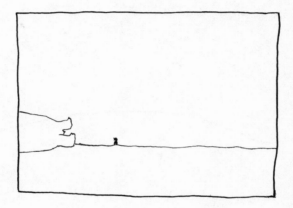

. . . the baby was dead.

The tiny boy cried tiny tears from his tiny face.

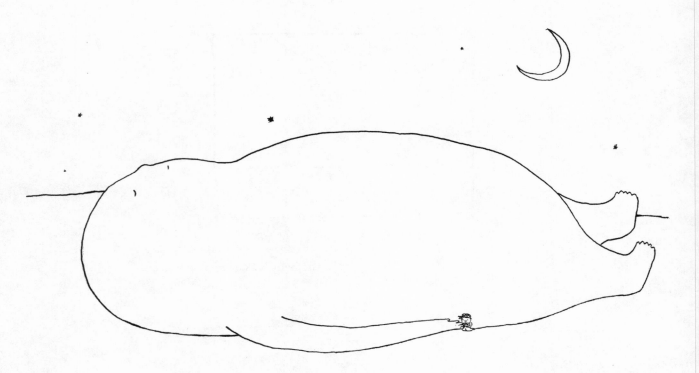

Ashamed of his tears, he hid his tiny face inside the giant's giant face.

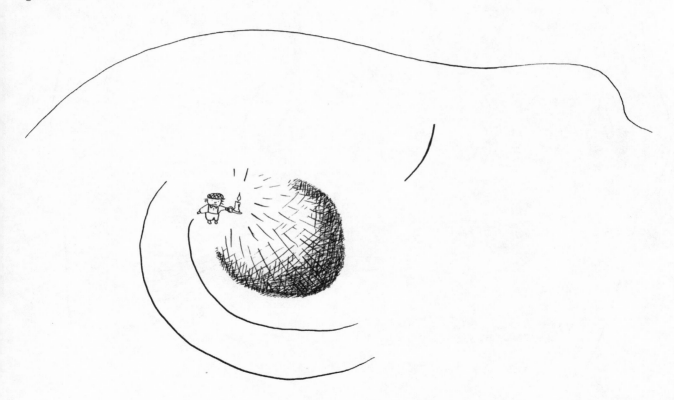

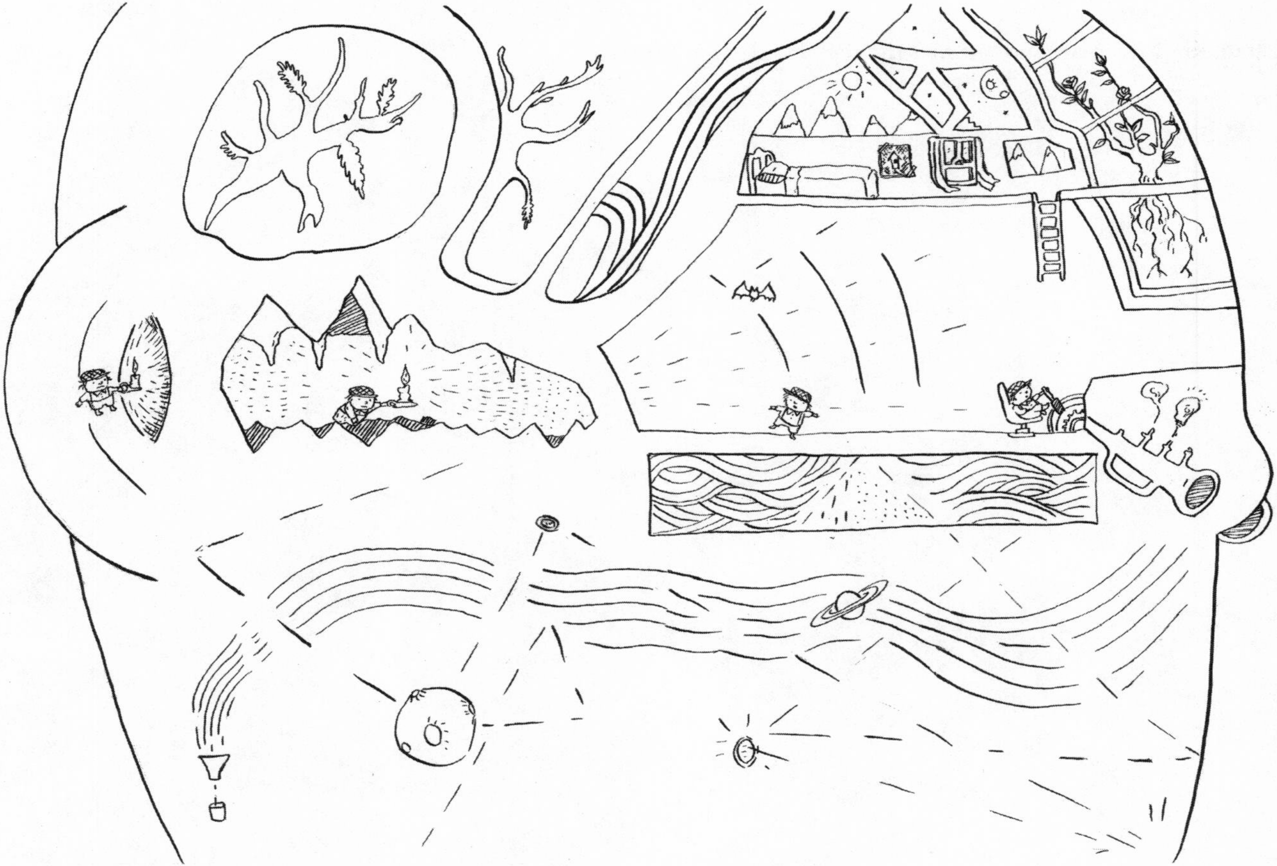

The boy decided to move the giant
toward the ocean to give him a proper burial.

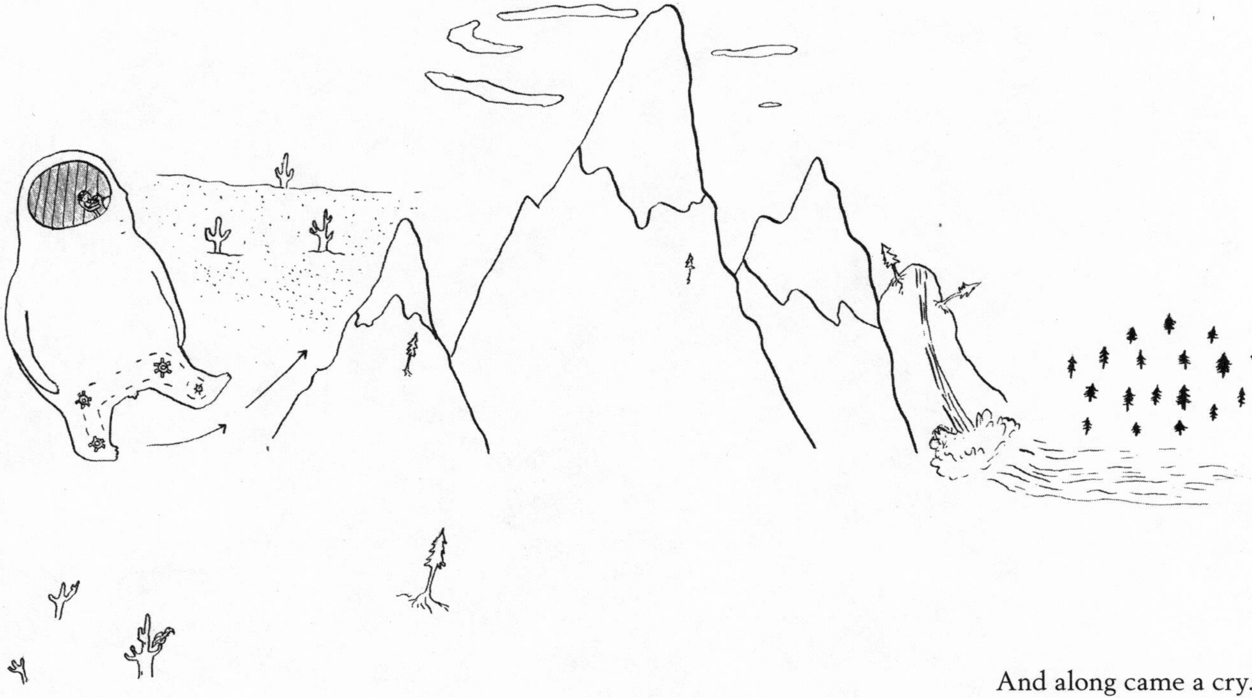

And along came a cry.

It was Old Ms. Jenkins.

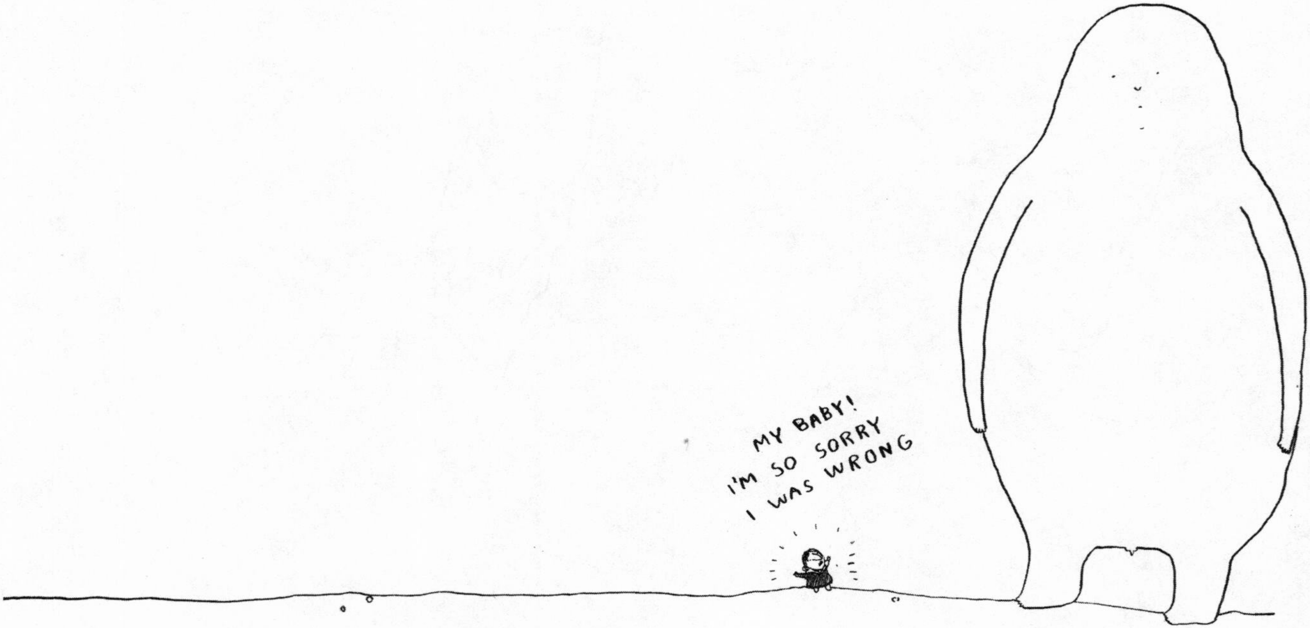
MY BABY!
I'M SO SORRY
I WAS WRONG

But it was too late.

"I'm sorry, I'm not your son."

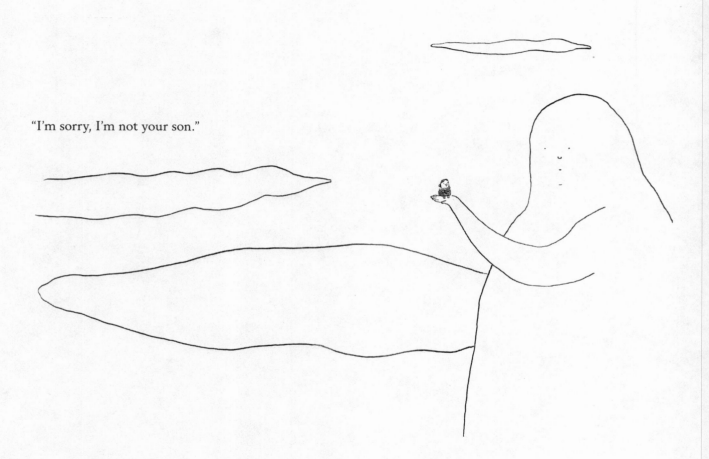

At first she didn't believe him, but she looked into his eyes and knew he was telling the truth.

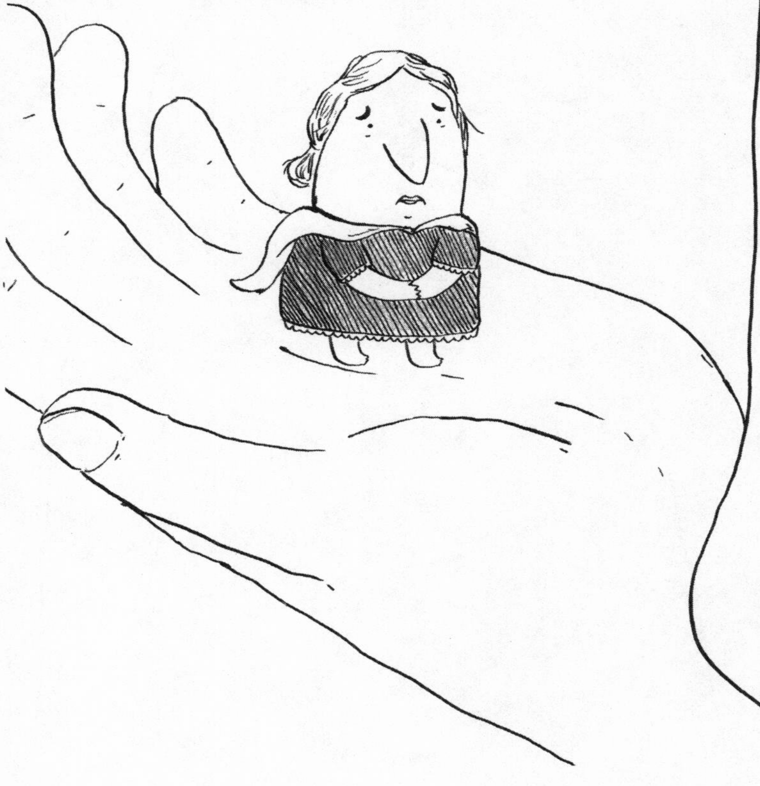

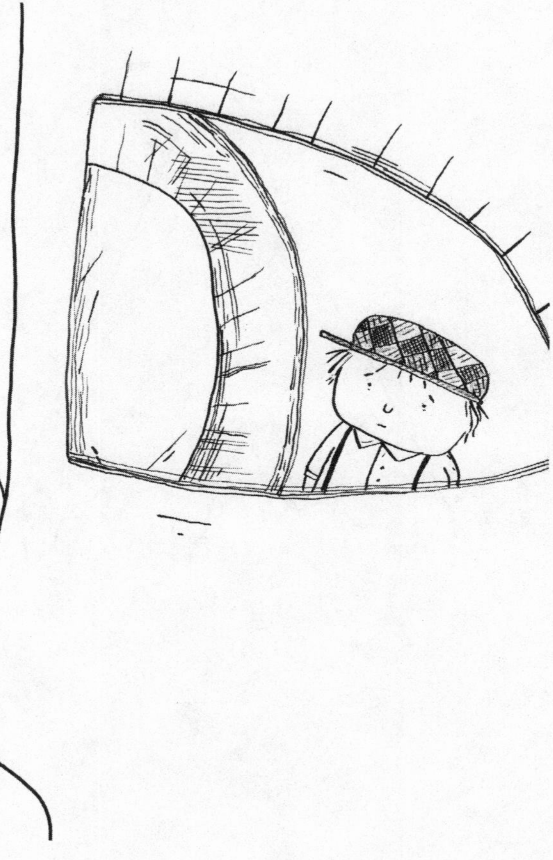

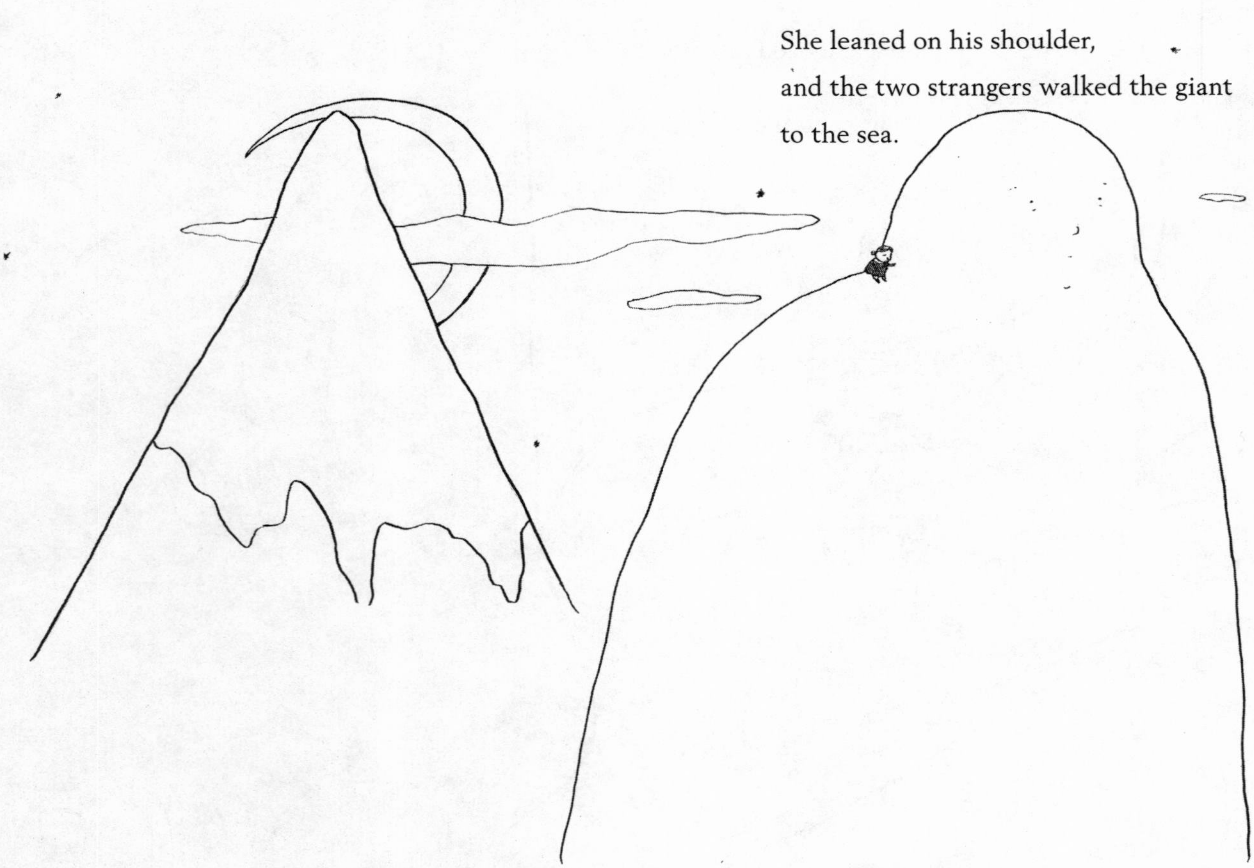

She leaned on his shoulder,
and the two strangers walked the giant
to the sea.

The end.

Which one is my head:

This egg? Or my head?

BERNARD THE SAILOR

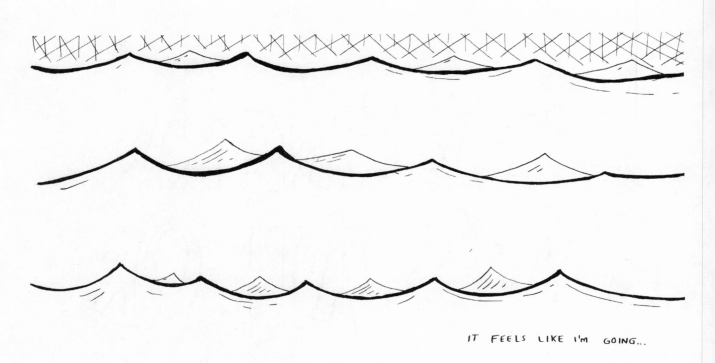

IT FEELS LIKE I'M GOING...

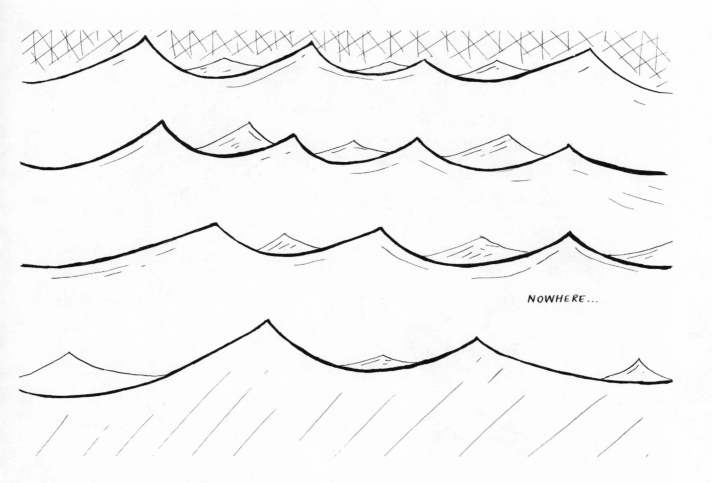

NOWHERE...

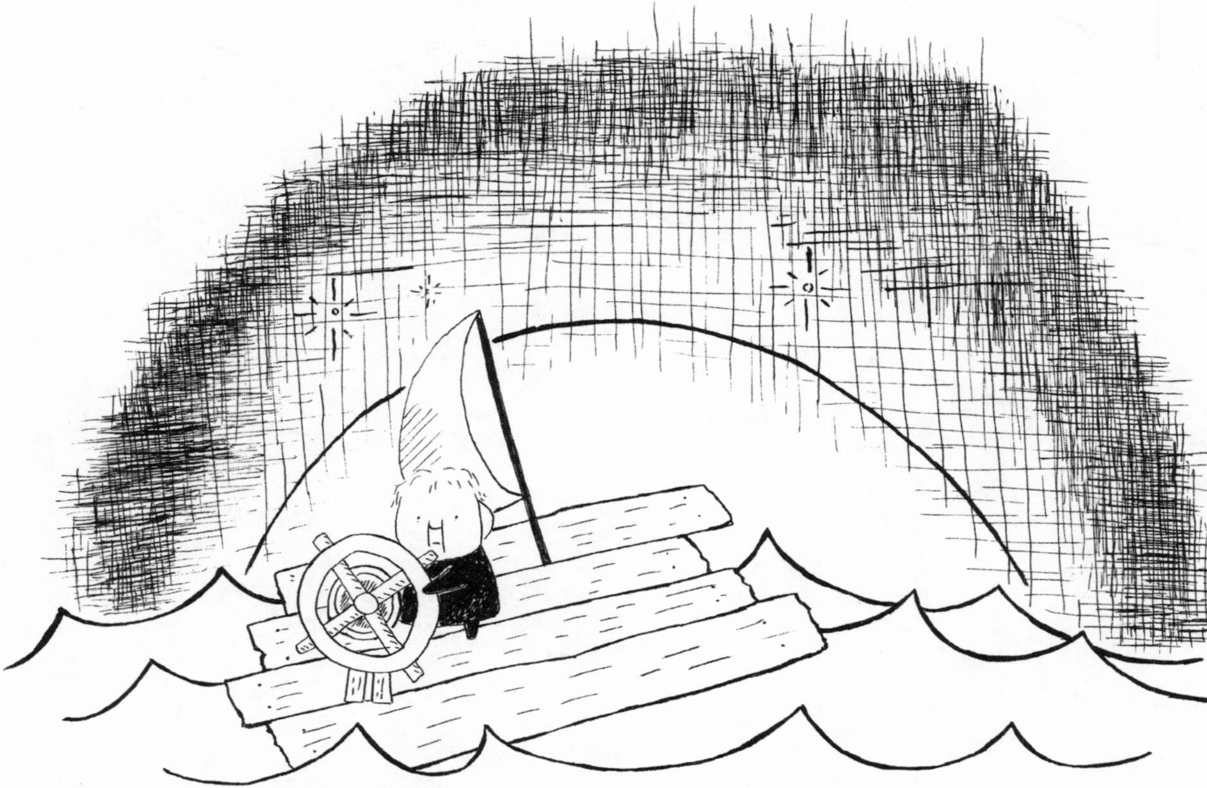

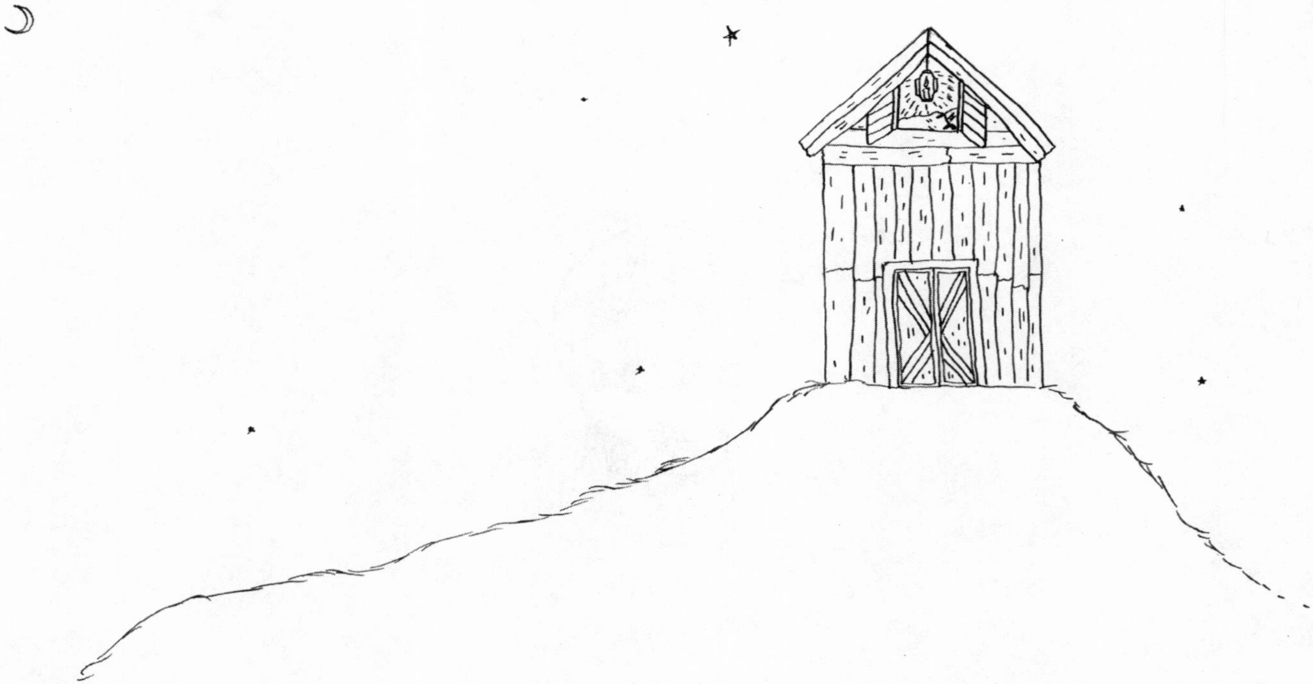

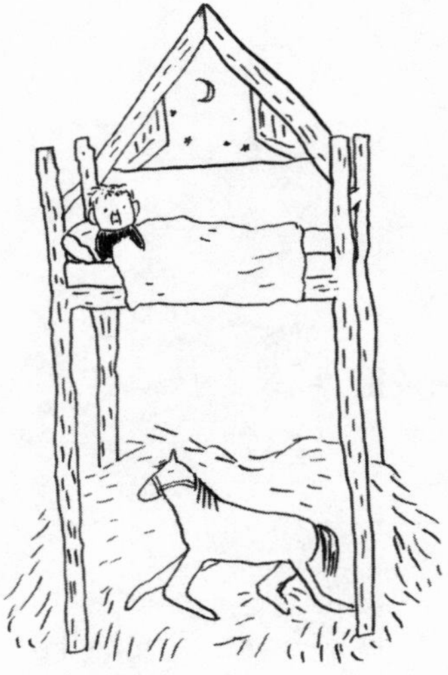

Bernard had woken up from a bad dream, only to realize he was living it: Bernard felt stuck.

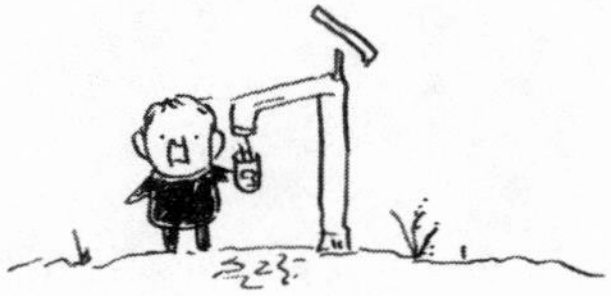

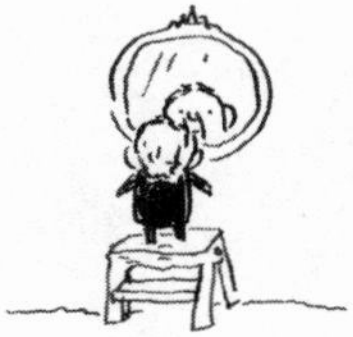

Every day he ordered the same thing at the same place, hoping that would make people remember him.

"I'll have my usual."

"And what would that be?" asked the waiter.

"Two eggs and some tea please."

"Mmhmm . . ."

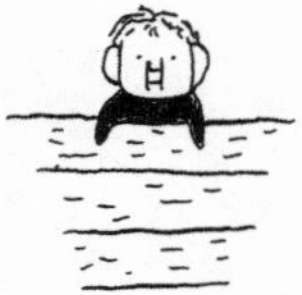

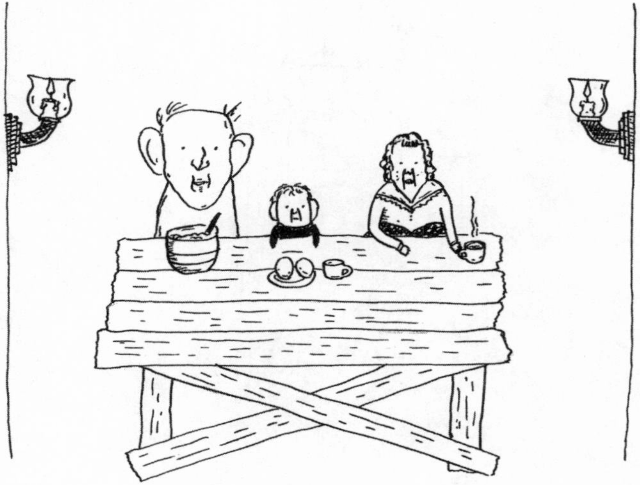

Bernard didn't feel special in his life. He worked at a modest pillow factory.

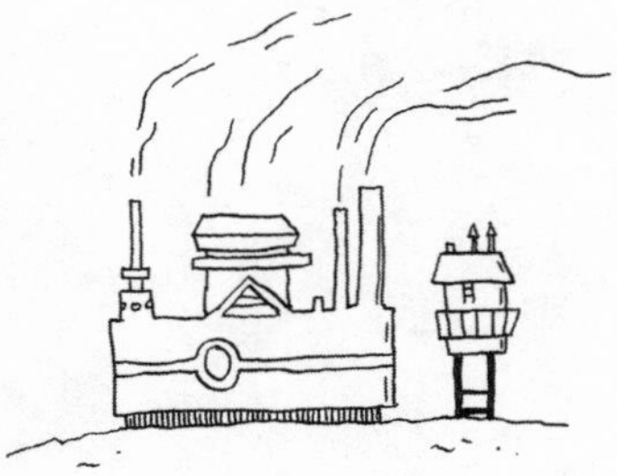

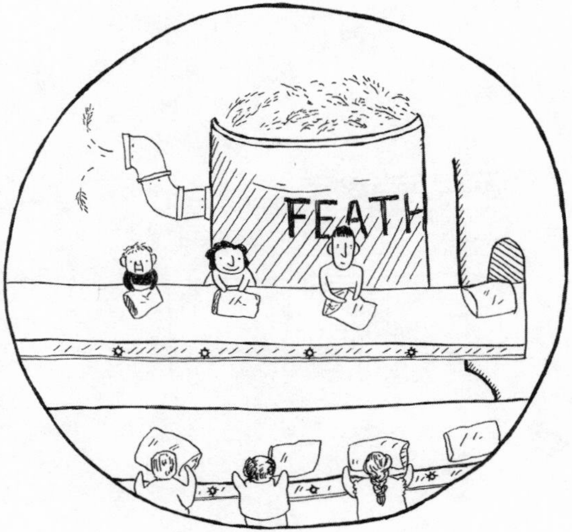
FEATH

And with every pillow he stuffed with feathers, the emptier he felt inside.

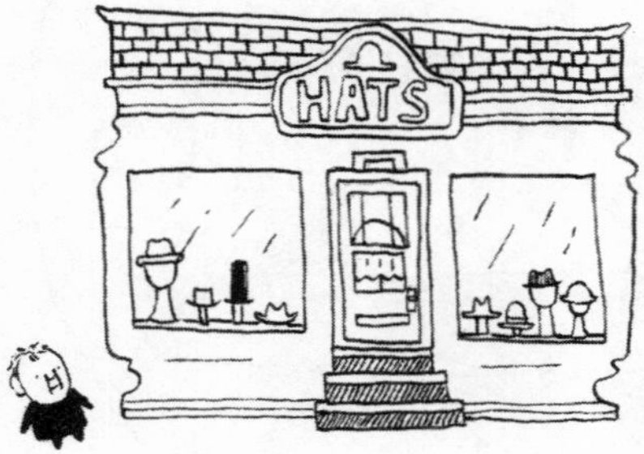
HATS

Bernard was a man of pride. He wanted to look good and feel good. He often daydreamed about owning a tall hat and all the amazing qualities that come with it—like power, respect, and mysteriousness.

He was a hard worker and saved up for eight years but still Bernard couldn't afford the tallest hat in the world. So he succumbed to other strategies . . .

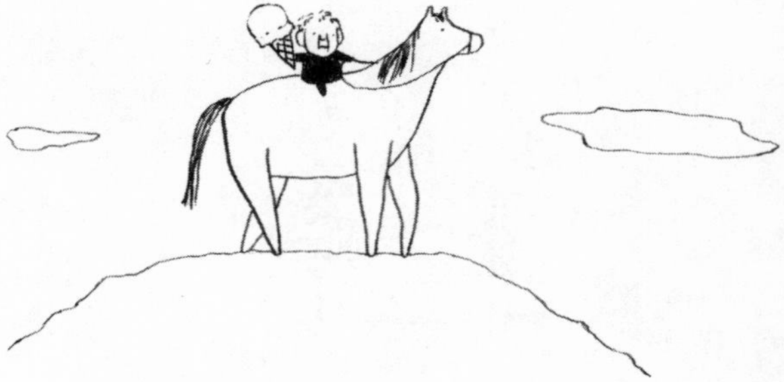

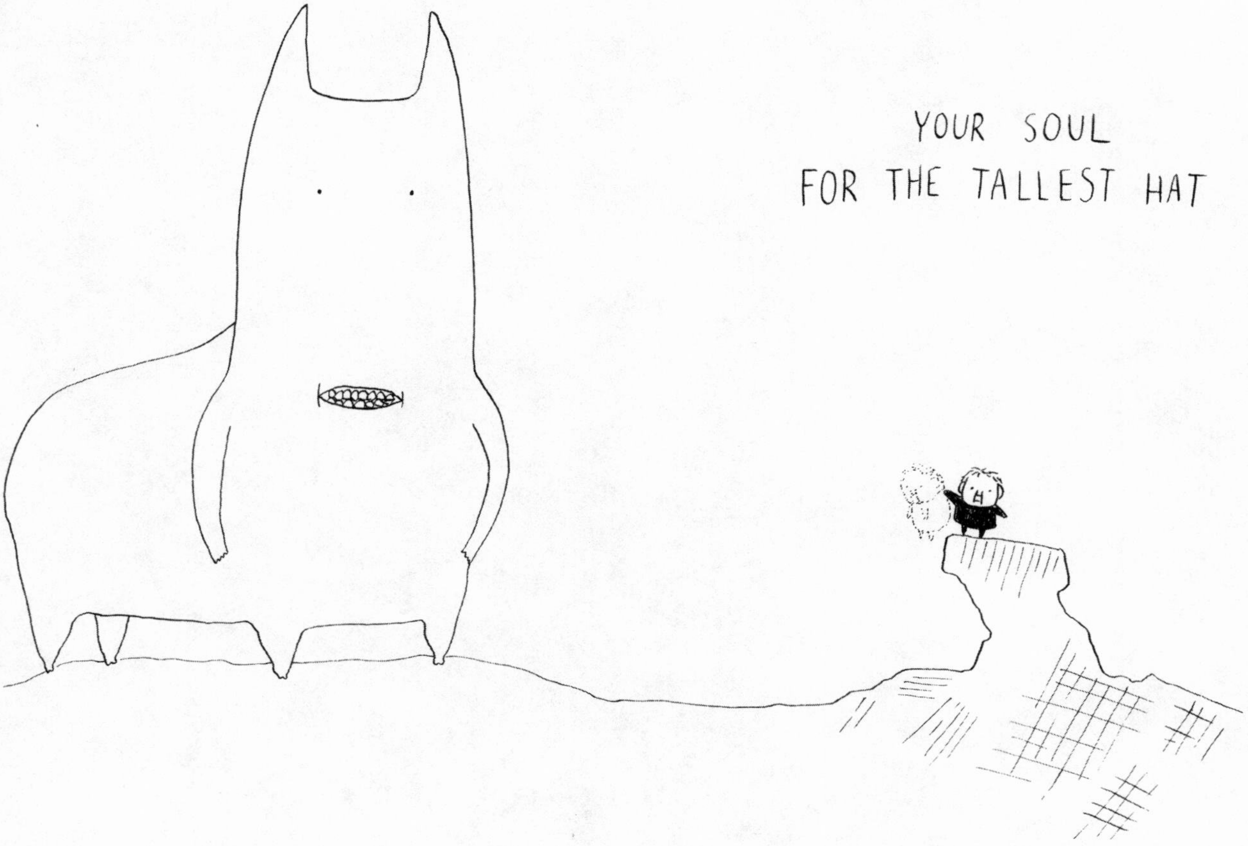
YOUR SOUL
FOR THE TALLEST HAT

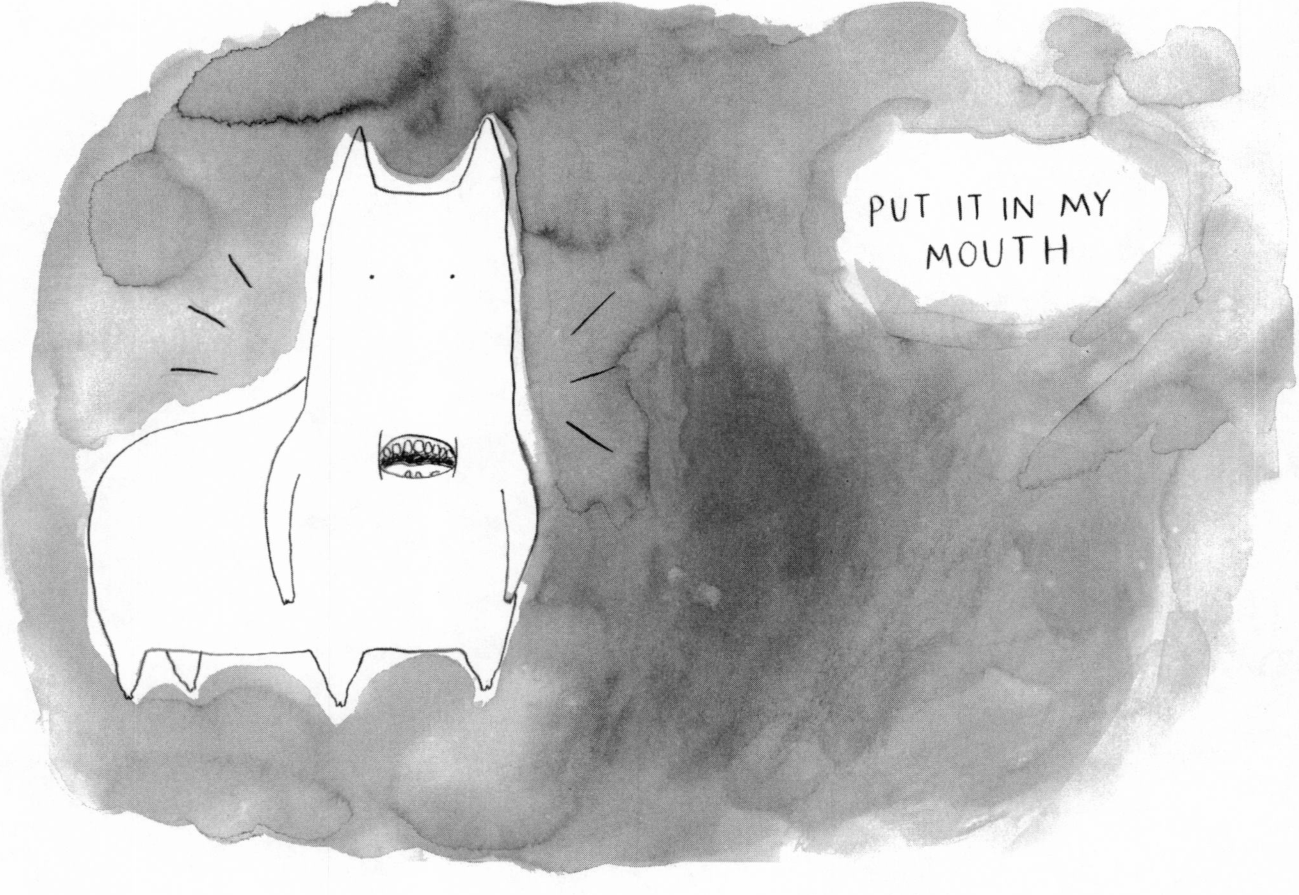
PUT IT IN MY MOUTH

Bernard loved his new hat.

He was excited to show it off.

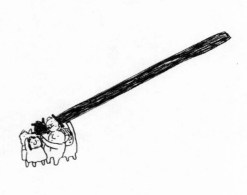

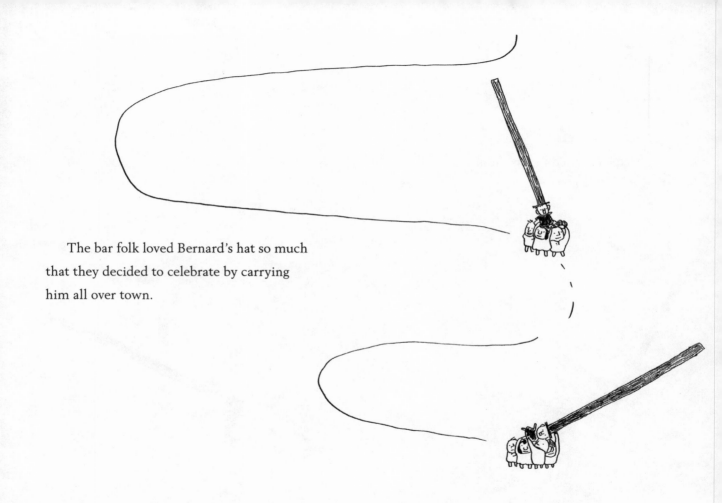

The bar folk loved Bernard's hat so much
that they decided to celebrate by carrying
him all over town.

They passed the time shop. Through
the window Bernard saw the pretty lady
he was secretly in love with. He had
been enamored with her just about as long
as he had been with his hat: eight strong years.

Bernard had never felt brave enough
to speak to her . . . til now.

"Here, put me down here please,"
Bernard politely requested.

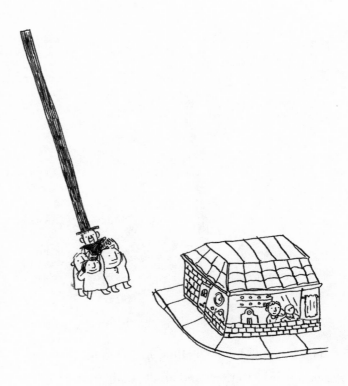

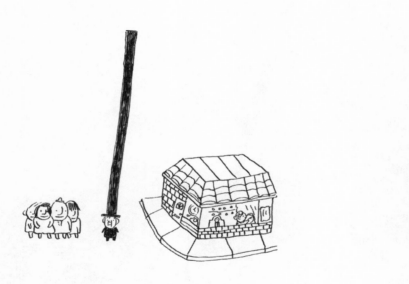

His fans stood there smiling and waiting.
Bernard turned to them and kindly said, "Thank
you, I can take it from here." And they left him to it.

Bernard's hat wouldn't fit through the door. His heart grew heavy with concern. How could he ever win the affection of the beautiful woman without his hat? He tried not to worry. He removed his hat, hugged it close and took the deepest breath he had ever taken in his life . . .

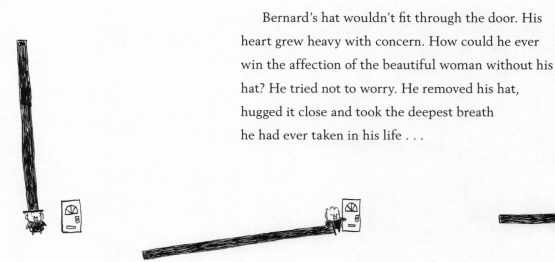

"Hi."

"Oh, hi."

Bernard tried to conjure something else to say, "Want to see me with my hat on? I'm handsome."

The girl laughed, "What?"

"I mean—people really love my hat. Come outside and see it on my head."

"I can see it from here, thank you."

"Wait!" He ran outside.

He delicately placed it onto the crown of his head and pointed, "Nice huh? You've gotta come outside and see the whole thing!"

"PUH-LEEEEZZE," he pleaded.

She sighed and stepped outside. She stared and nodded, "You're right. It is a nice hat."

And just like that a gust of wind blew it right off Bernard's head and into the sky. The woman could not help but laugh. And off they went chasing the tallest hat in the world.

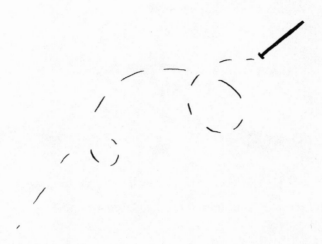

"I'm Ellie by the way!"

"I'm Bernard, it's a pleasure to finally meet
you." He ran and smiled through the misery of his
hat mishap. And then . . . the hat flew completely
out of sight.

Bernard looked through his telescope but could not spot his hat anywhere.

He thought, "Maybe I'm looking through this wrong!" and flipped the telescope around.

Ellie moved closer to Bernard and leaned into the eyepiece. "Oh my!" She stepped back startled.

"What? What'd you see?"

"Nothing . . ." replied Ellie.

INSIDE BERNARD:

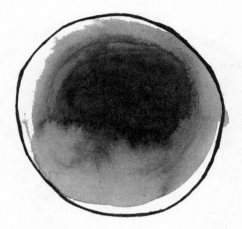

He stared at her, uncertain of what to think.

"Okay my turn. It's only fair."

He flipped the telescope and gazed into it. Bernard
had no idea the telescope was powerful enough
to look into the pit of Ellie's soul . . . which was glowing,
full of beauty and magic.

INSIDE ELLIE:

" . . . So when you said you saw nothing, you weren't kidding."

Ellie nodded, she played with her locket, she was nervous, "Where's your soul?"

He sighed and sat on a rock. Embarrassed he slipped his words under his breath, " . . . I sold it to the Devil."

"Can you get it back?" asked Ellie.

"I traded it for the hat . . ." Bernard couldn't even look at her.

Ellie put her hand on his shoulder, "Don't you worry, we'll find it together. And then you'll get your soul back!"

"C'mon, I think it flew this way," Ellie pointed.

They both jumped into the water and made their way into the Swamp.

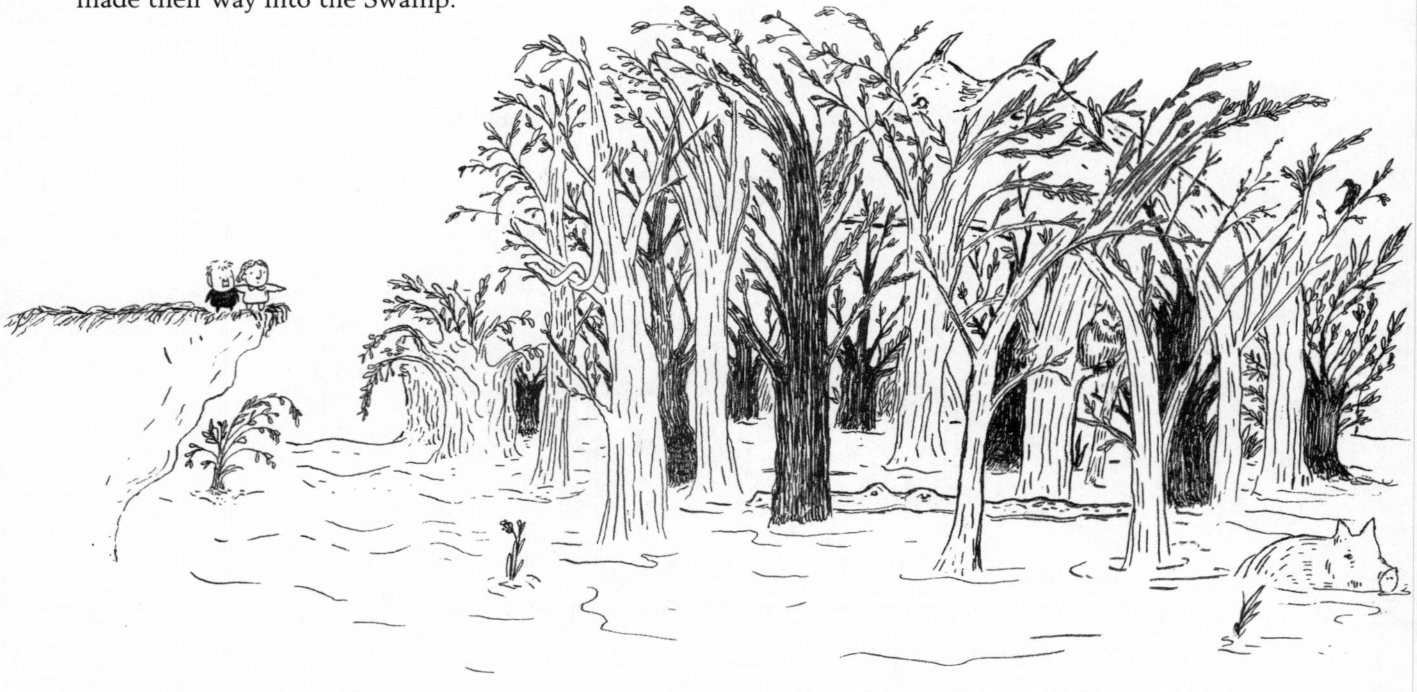

They asked the Ancient Frog, guardian of the Swamp, if he had seen Bernard's hat.

"So it was YOUR very tall hat that made me choke!" he croaked.

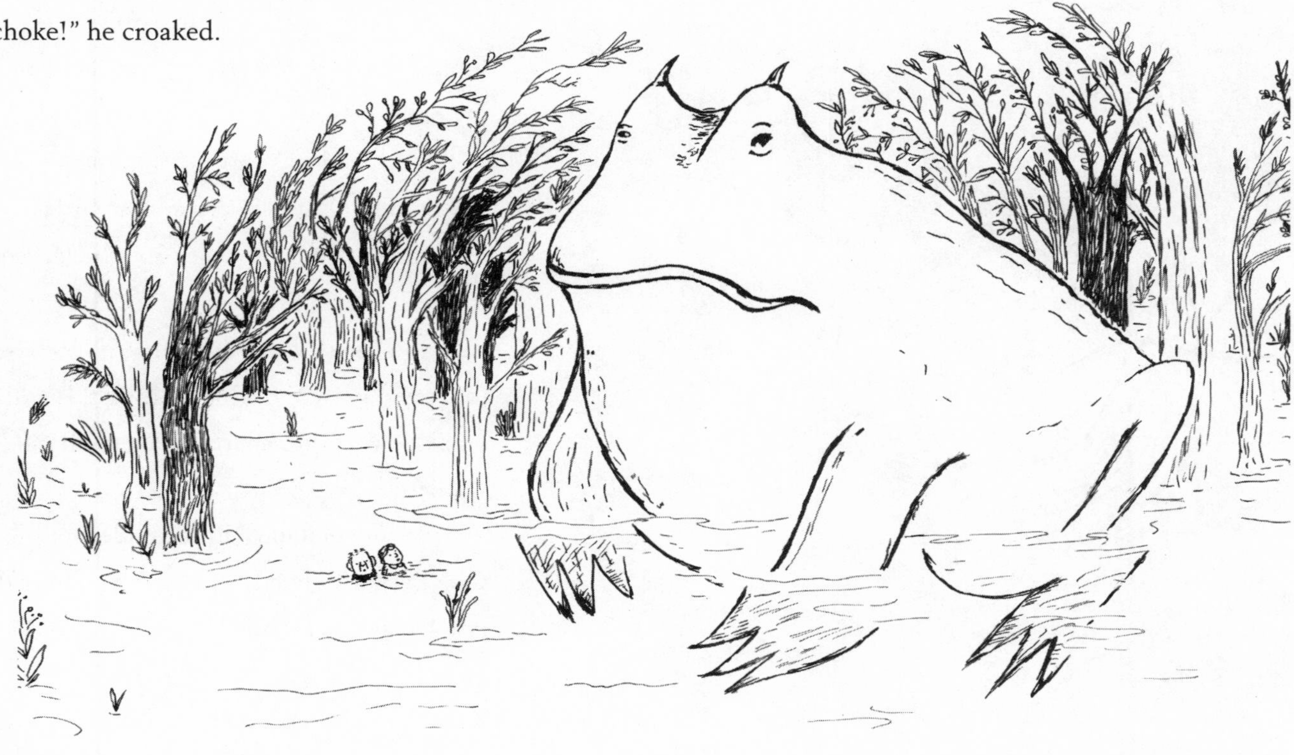

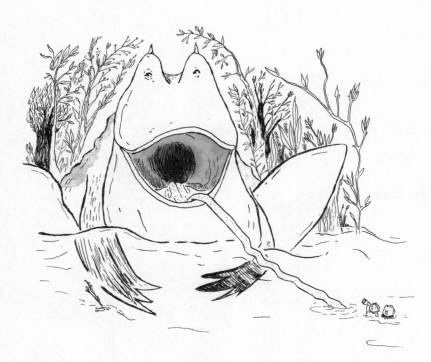

"Yes, the wind took it from me! I did not mean for you to choke on it," bowed Bernard.

The Frog croaked again, "You are forgiven. You may retrieve your hat from my belly."

"WAIT! How can we trust you're not just trying to eat us?!" asked Bernard.

Ellie took out the telescope, "I can see it! But it's far."

"You have exactly fifteen minutes before my digestion begins, or my acids will break your bodies apart and you will die," warned the Frog.

"We understand," Ellie nodded and took Bernard's hand, and up they climbed into the Frog's mouth.

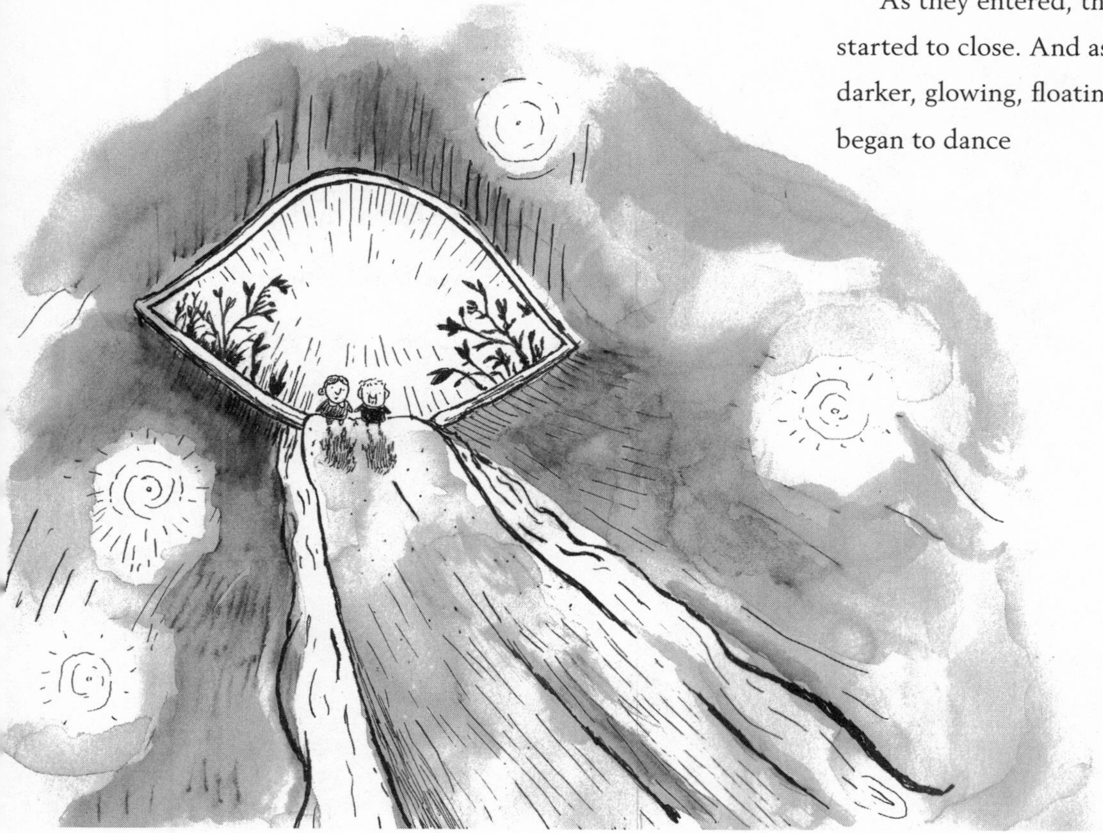

As they entered, the Frog's mouth started to close. And as it got darker, glowing, floating lights began to dance

. . . fireflies.

A firefly floated toward them, "Hey kids, heard about your mission. Hop on my back and let's lickety-split outta here before the bile comes!"

"What's in it for you?" asked Bernard.

"HA. I wanna help because I can! Wouldn't you? My life span's almost over—least I can do is spend it doing something meaningful."

"Thank you so much for your kindness," Ellie replied.

"Of course little lady. C'mon, let's play with fire!"

They flew through the wild winds of the
Ancient Frog's breath, but the winds were too
strong, and they lost control, crashing right
into a web.

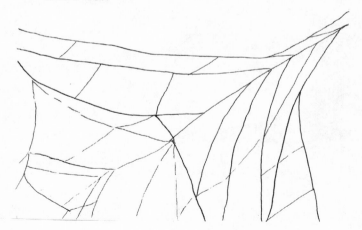

They crashed into the web of a cathedral. A praying mantis rubbed his hands together and smiled.

"I had prayed for more company . . . I've been alone for so long," whispered the Praying Mantis as he untied them from the web.

Bernard scratched his chin, "How long have you been here?"

"Ninety-seven days . . ."

"What? But how? The bile . . ."

"I've been drinking the bile
and praying to the Gods to make me
immune to it. And they have blessed
me and I have been able to sustain life
down here. Come, I can save you. Pray
and drink with me."

The Praying Mantis brought a
glass of green liquid.

"What happened to these guys?"
Bernard pointed to bodies of insects
lying on the ground with spilled cups.

"Not everyone becomes immune. The Gods choose. Now it is time for your test . . ." He moved closer with the bile in his shaking hand.

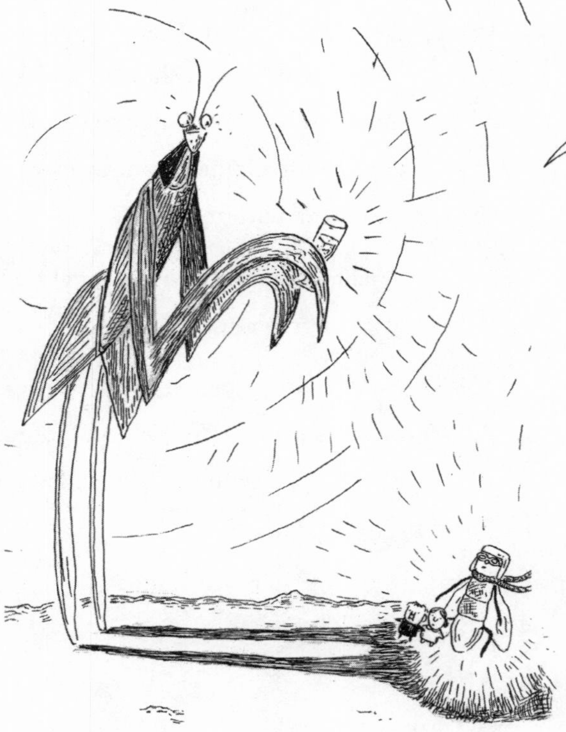

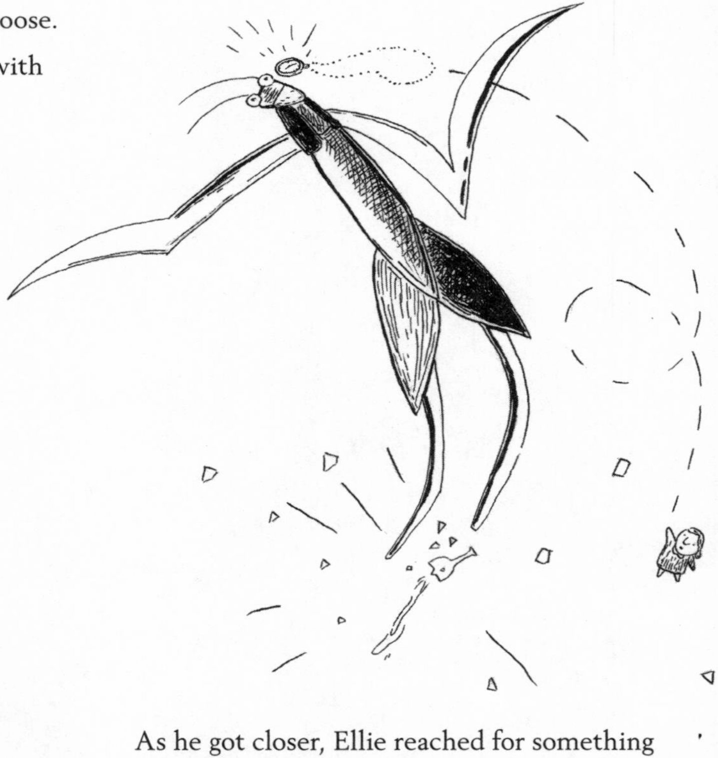

As he got closer, Ellie reached for something and chucked it at his head, knocking the Praying Mantis out cold on the floor.

They made a run for it but when Bernard looked back,
Ellie had gone back to pick up something. She caught up,
and the three friends continued their journey.

"What'd you go back for?" asked Bernard.

She opened her hand, and in it was a locket. "My
father gave me this watch before he passed . . . I'm
sentimental."

"I understand. Thank you for helping me find my hat."

They both smiled. But the pulsating tick of her watch washed it away. "The bile is coming . . ."

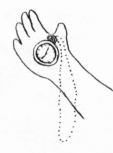

The Firefly twirled and danced, dodging the falling beads of bile. But alas, this dance could not go on forever. A few droplets hit his glowing bulb.

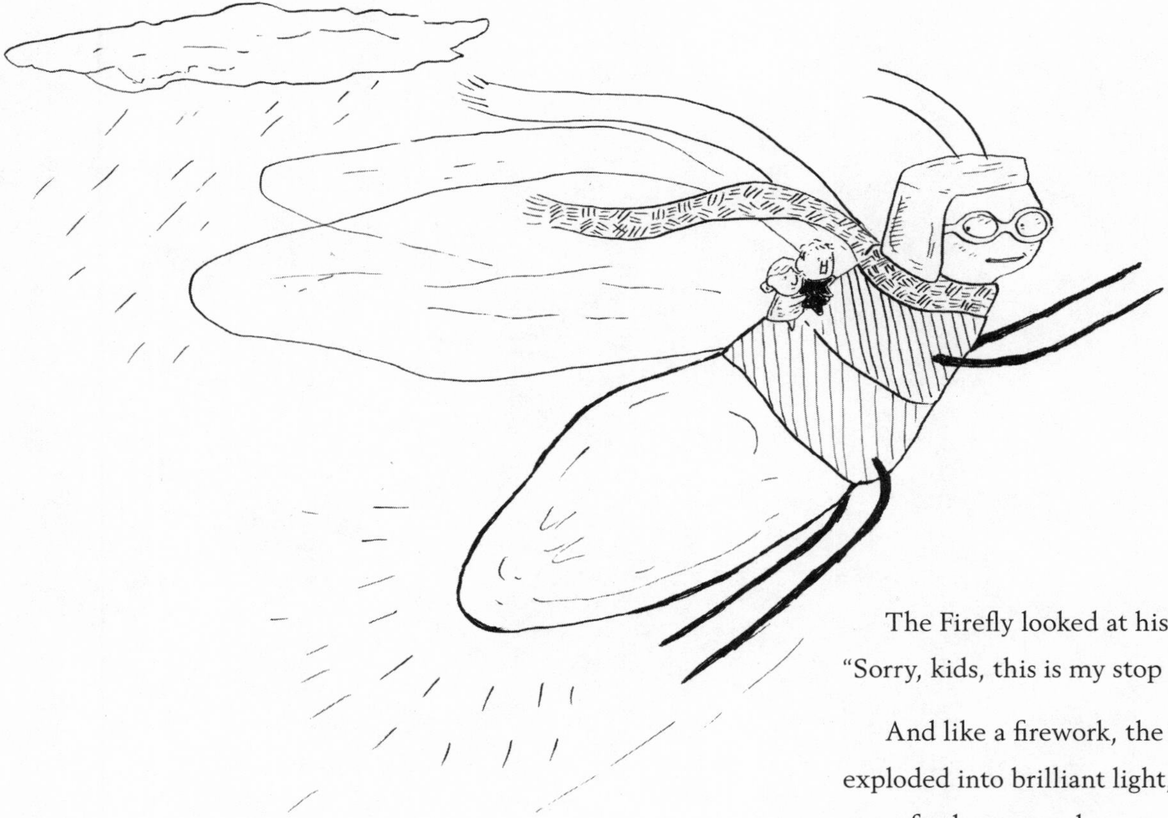

The Firefly looked at his friends. "Sorry, kids, this is my stop . . ."

And like a firework, the Firefly exploded into brilliant light, shooting rays of color everywhere.

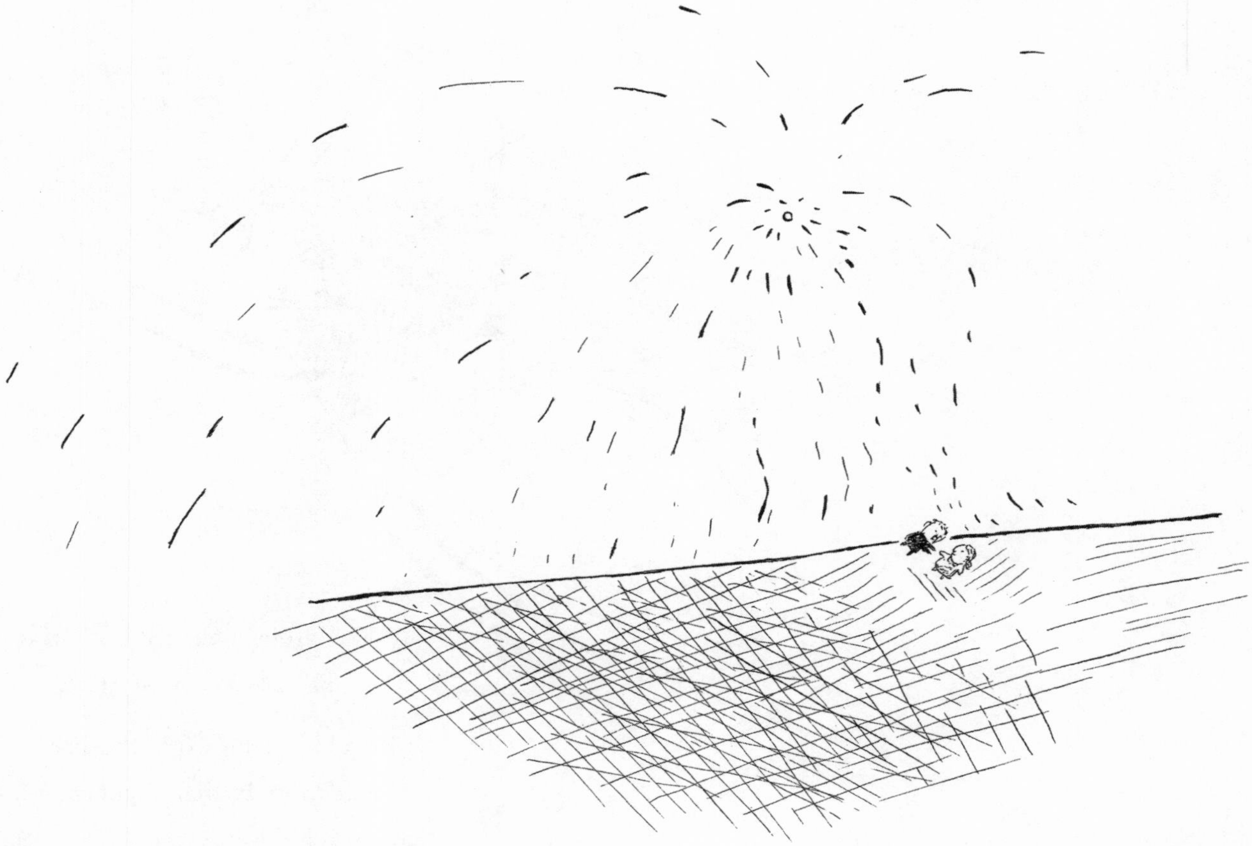

The glowing sparkles rained onto Ellie and
Bernard and they began to glow.

The wind whispered, "I'm with you
now . . . Good luck my friends."

They walked toward what seemed
like the end . . . and then they saw it . . .

. . . the tallest hat in the world!

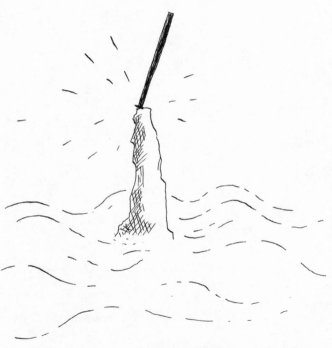

"Let's do this . . ." Bernard took Ellie's
hand.

He climbed to the top. Bernard couldn't believe he was on a date with Ellie. He wondered if she knew it was a date too. He thought, "I bet I look really cool right now. I wonder if Ellie thinks so too." He turned to see her, but when he turned he saw a giant wave of bile rise and take her down. Bernard's heart leapt.

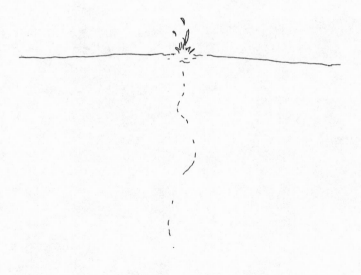

"Bernard! You came back for me!" Ellie
kissed him on the cheek. "Oh Bernard,
you should've saved yourself."

He stared at her longingly, "I guess I'm sentimental too."

Bernard took her hand. They held each other well.

"You may not have a soul, but you have a beautiful heart," whispered Ellie.

Their hearts ached. As the bile seeped in so did the realization of knowing this was their last moment together. An old record player sat the bottom of the Frog's belly and it began to play a sad tune.

"Dance with me," Bernard said. Ellie nodded and they slow danced.

The bile started to take Ellie, she was growing weak and fell into his arms. "What does Heaven look like?"

"Brilliant sun shining onto golden glowing grass . . . and there's a little cottage big enough for the two of us, with a clothesline for our little clothes. And a tall, tall swing that hangs from the moon up in the sky where I push you . . . and you laugh . . . because we're happy together."

Bernard and Ellie began to fade into particles.

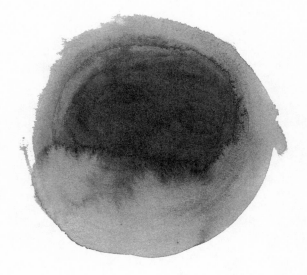

And then there was darkness.

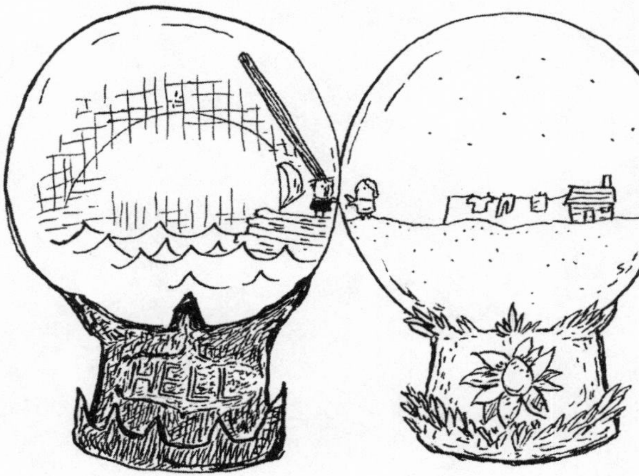
HELL

The end.

MEET ME AGAIN

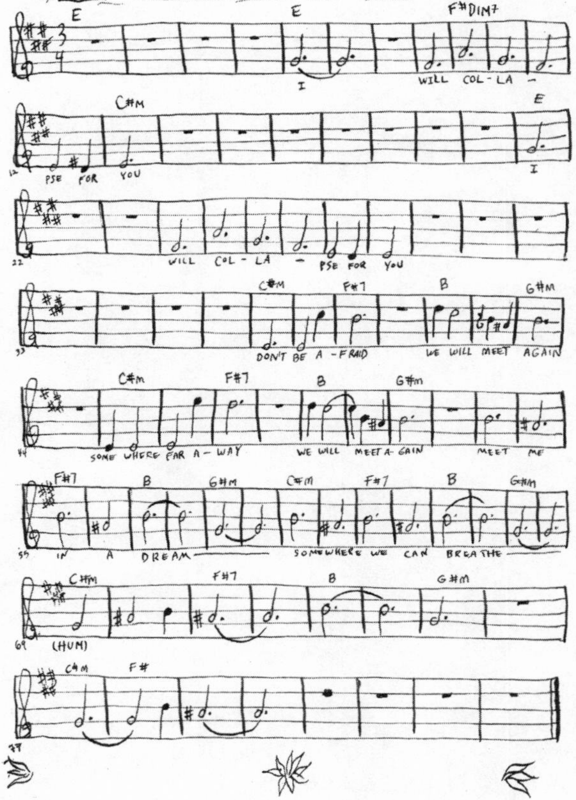
E E F#DIM7
I WILL COL-LA-
C#M E
PSE FOR YOU I
WILL COL-LA-PSE FOR YOU
C#M F#7 B G#M
DON'T BE A-FRAID WE WILL MEET AGAIN
C#m F#7 B G#m
SOME WHERE FAR A-WAY WE WILL MEET A-GAIN MEET ME
F#7 B G#M C#M F#7 B G#M
IN A DREAM SOMEWHERE WE CAN BREATHE
C#M F#7 B G#M
(HUM)
C#M F#

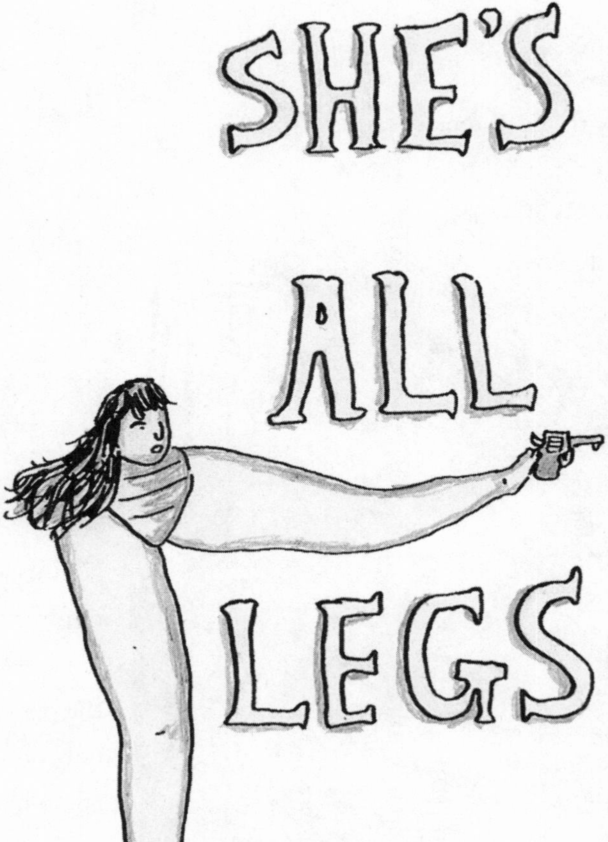
SHE'S
ALL
LEGS

Donald's fingers crawled across the bed like a
tiny soldier. They approached my thighs; I took
a deep breath and turned over. I pretended to
be asleep so Donald would resign his affection.
And he did. Quickly he met his slumber,
turned, and stole the blanket that
was covering our distant
bodies.

I tried to remember a time when
the world wasn't so crowded with
loneliness, a time when I could feel
the person lying next to me. But
our romance had expired. What
could have been love was nothing
but curdled milk. I miss all the
memories I can't remember.

I got out of bed and stared at the Moon.
Without words we commiserated. I could feel
the world breathing. It seemed winded—like
the unfortunate circumstances of reality
had hit the world right in its
gut when it wasn't
looking.

The Moon bid me farewell.
I folded my name into a whisper
and passed it along to her,
"It was nice to meet you, I'm
Agatha." I watched the sky
swallow her whole then roll
out the next shining ball of
light. It was morning so I
climbed back into bed.

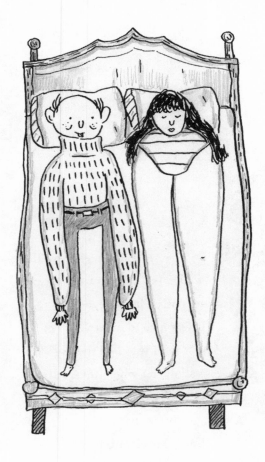

As soon as I closed my eyes, Donald opened his. He reached for the TV remote and turned it on. He always hyperventilates while laughing at cartoons. Breaking news interrupted his program and Donald let out a childlike "Aww man!" then noticed I was awake. Damn. The TV was small but the news was big.

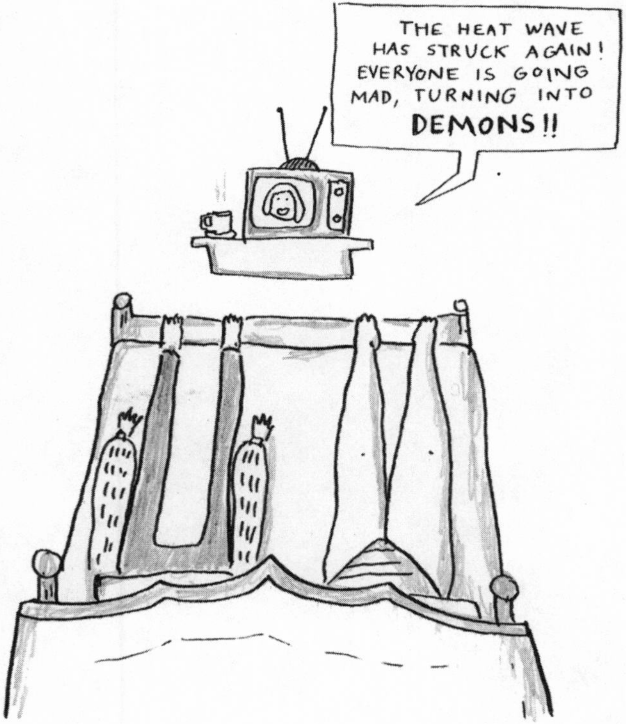
THE HEAT WAVE HAS STRUCK AGAIN! EVERYONE IS GOING MAD, TURNING INTO DEMONS!!

The world was collapsing and so was my heart. I couldn't just lie there and watch it happen.

"BORING!!" nasalized Donald. He laughed at his own joke and turned off the TV. His lanky arms reached for me and pulled me right onto his chest. Things were getting too hot.

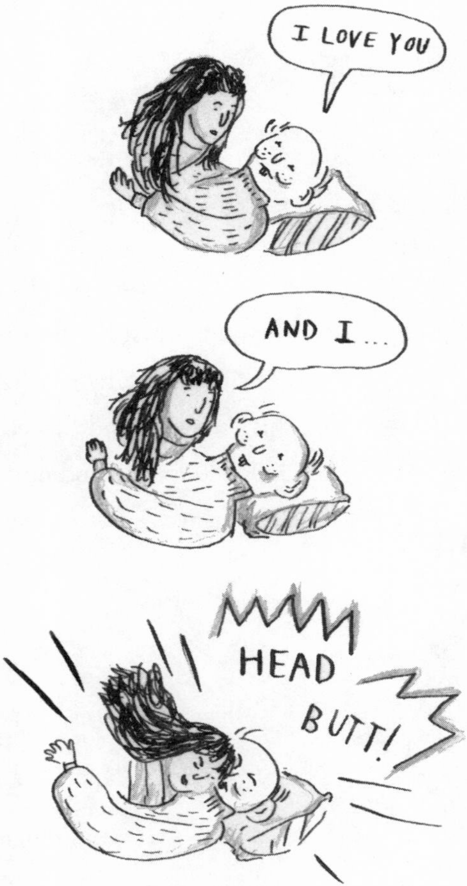
I LOVE YOU
AND I...
HEAD
BUTT!

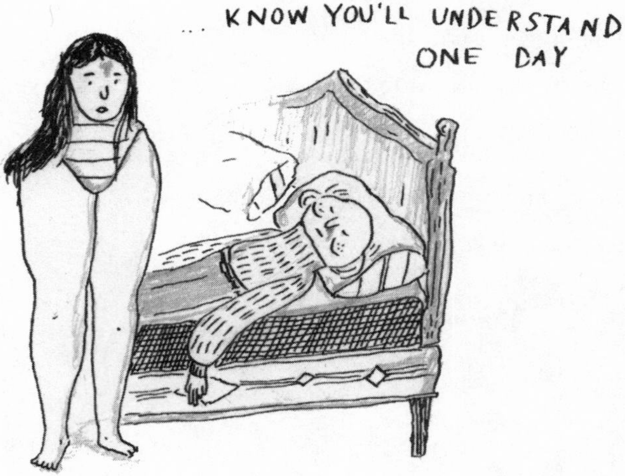
... KNOW YOU'LL UNDERSTAND ONE DAY

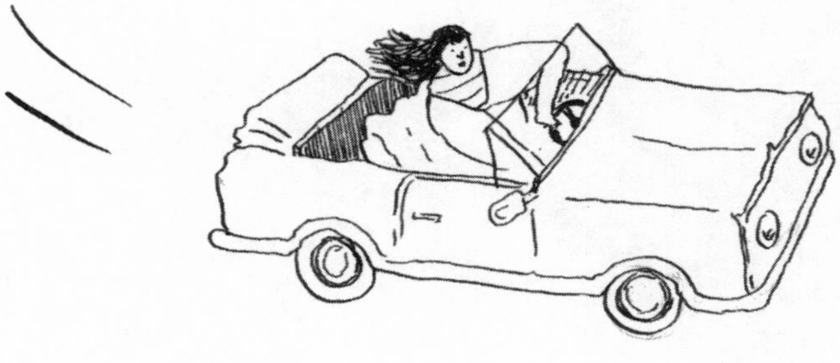

Murder and chaos wreaked havoc on our land. Hell was getting bigger. The bigger it got, the bigger the trouble there was on the streets. I couldn't just watch the world go down in flames.

My plan: To Kill the Devil and Save the World.

I kept hearing Donald's echoing voice, "I love you— I love you—I LOVE YOU . . ."

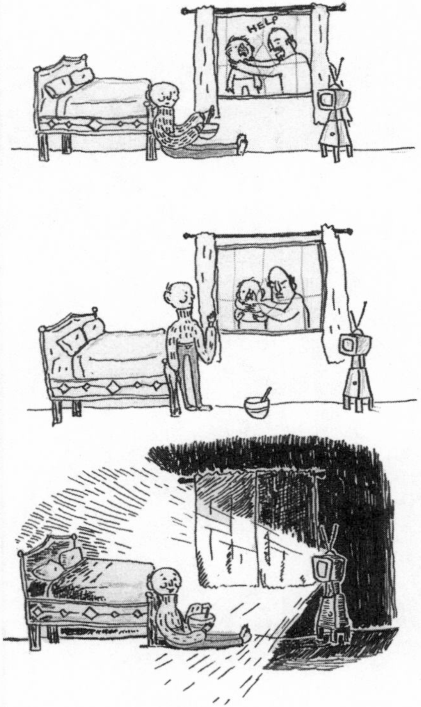
HELP

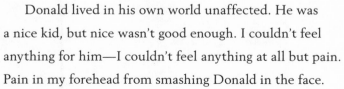

Donald lived in his own world unaffected. He was a nice kid, but nice wasn't good enough. I couldn't feel anything for him—I couldn't feel anything at all but pain. Pain in my forehead from smashing Donald in the face.

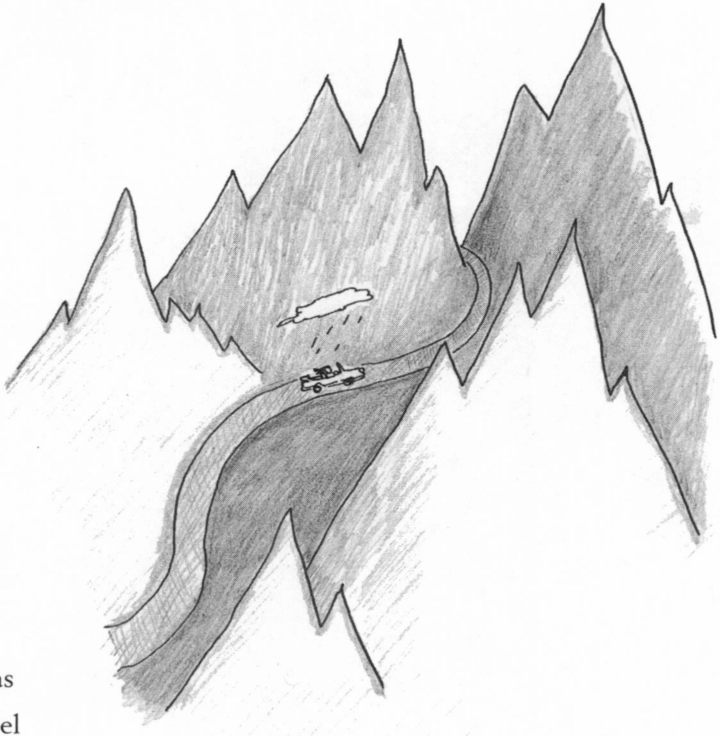

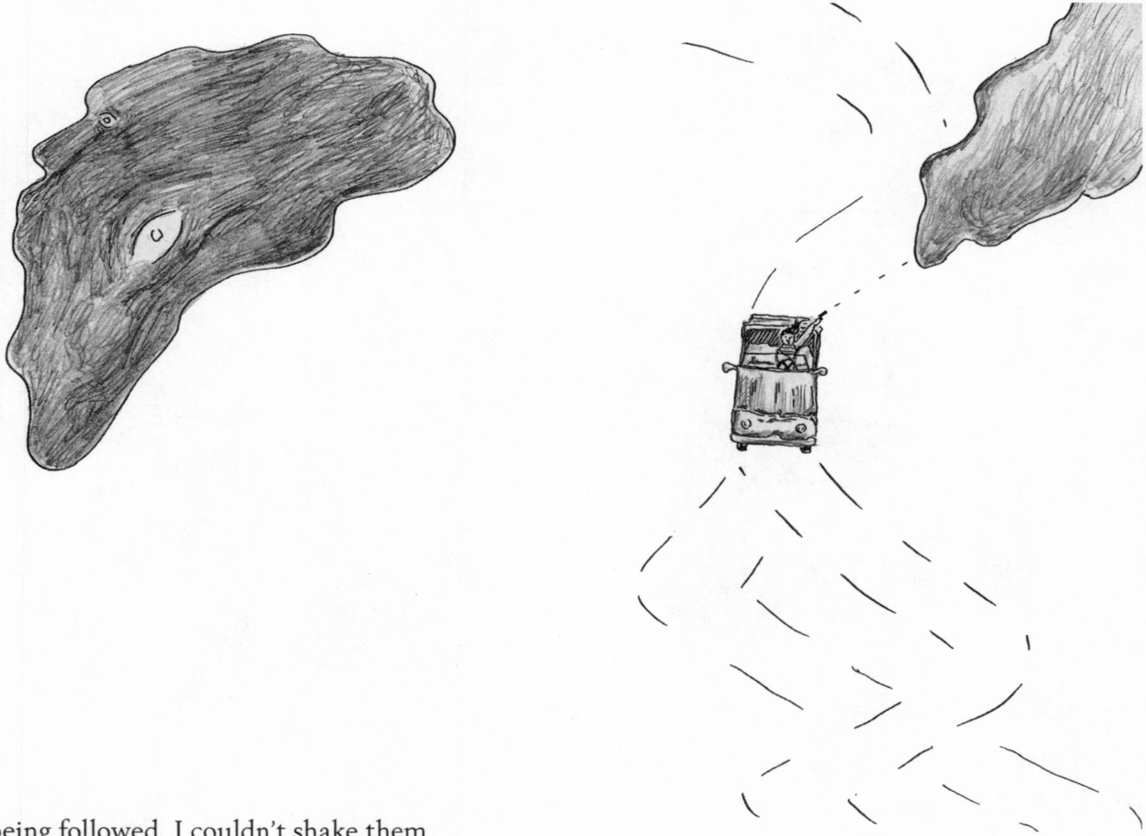

I was being followed. I couldn't shake them.

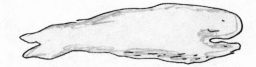

The clouds were made of ghosts of unfinished business. It was difficult to point my gun at them when they kept shape-shifting into things I recognized . . . My head was burning. Could I trust myself? Did I have a fever? Was I turning into a demon?

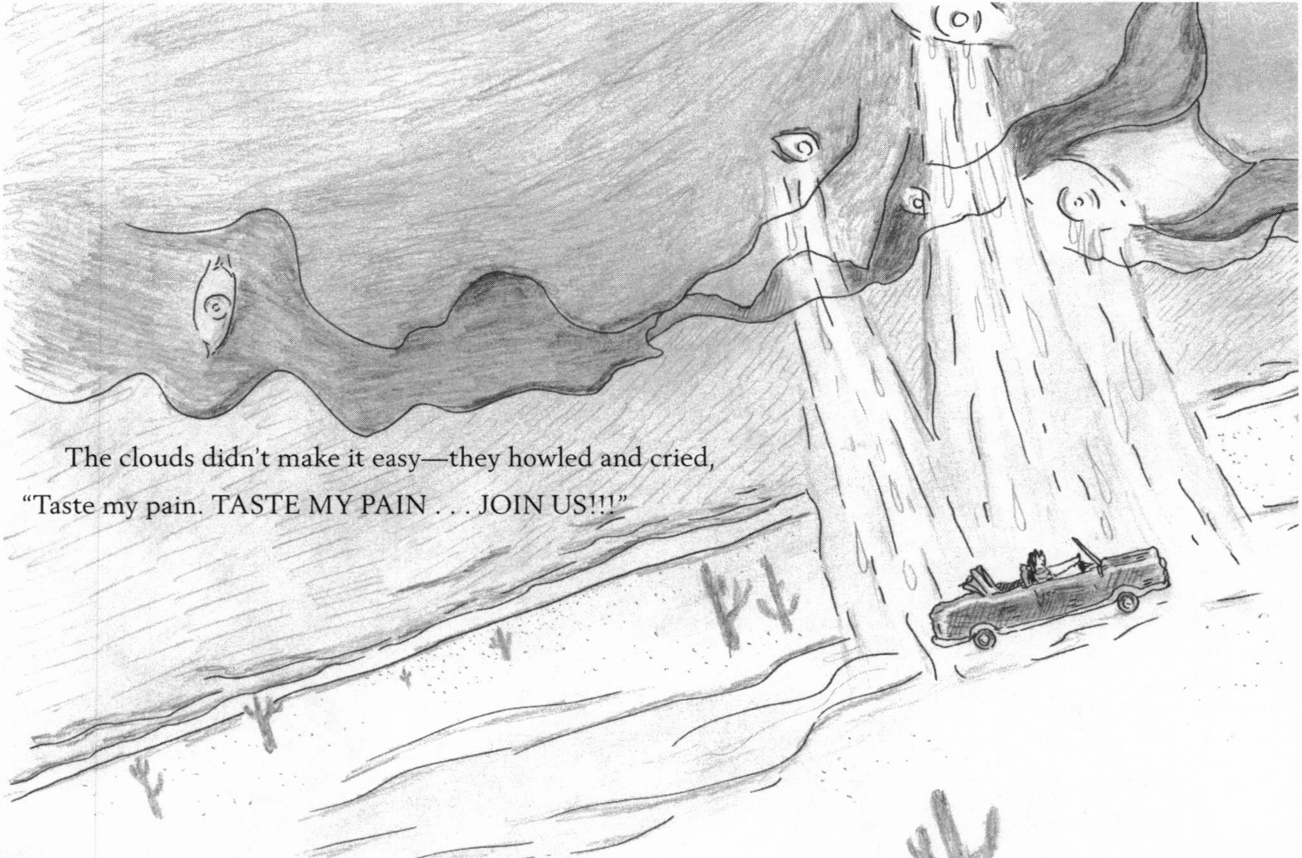

The clouds didn't make it easy—they howled and cried, "Taste my pain. TASTE MY PAIN . . . JOIN US!!!"

I reached for my pistol, shot, and punctured one of the clouds hovering over my head. The cloud's blood splashed all over my face. I had never killed anything before. I felt fine.

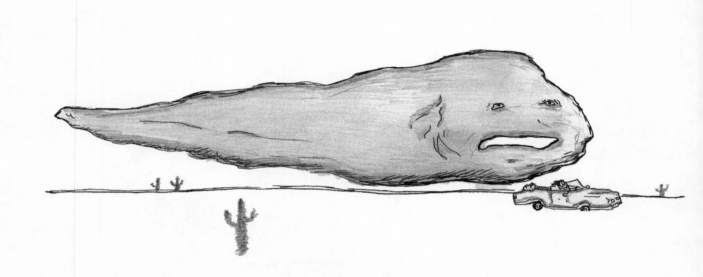

There were far too many so I retired my pistol.

My fever was getting worse. I had driven for hours straight with those goddamn clouds hovering over me. As I got closer to the shiny lights of Vegas, I felt myself slowly fading away.

And then . . . I was there. I WAS FINALLY SOMEWHERE WITH SHELTER! And just as I made it to the building, everything turned black . . .

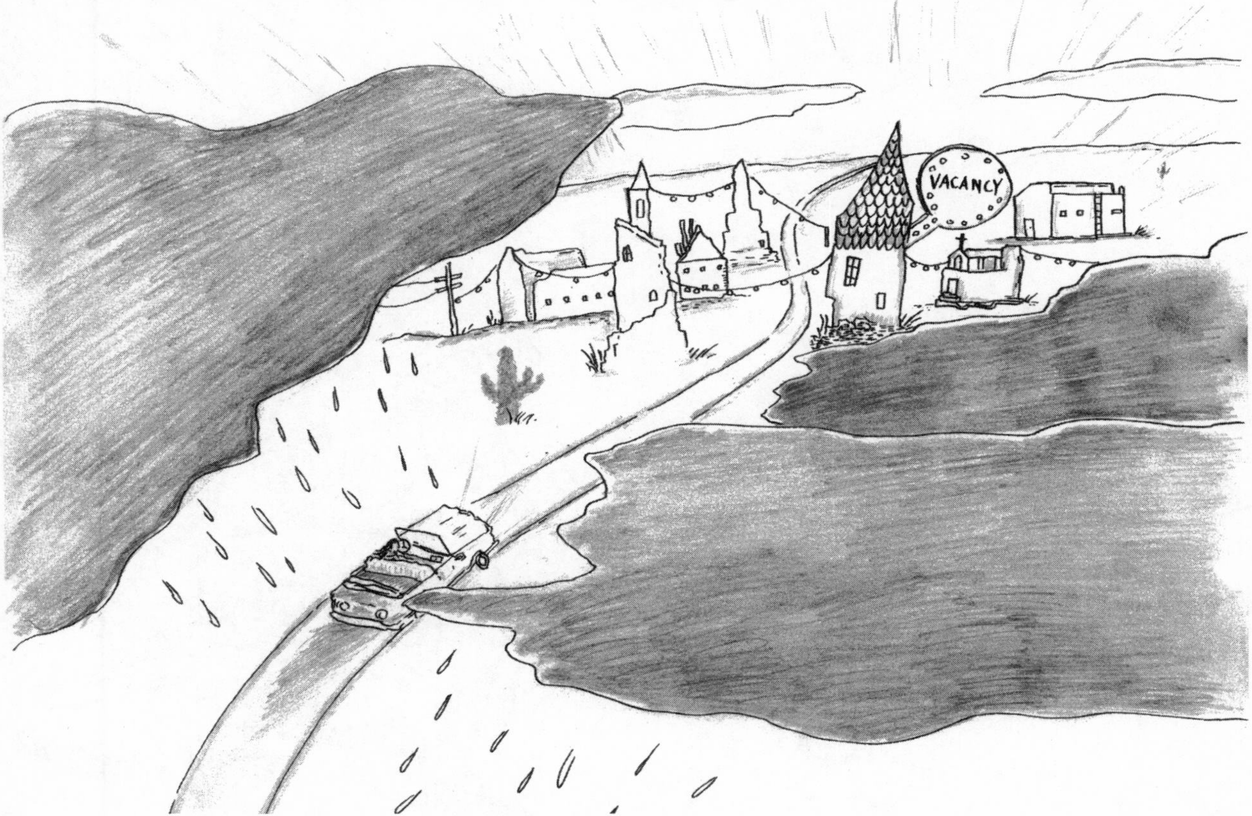
VACANCY

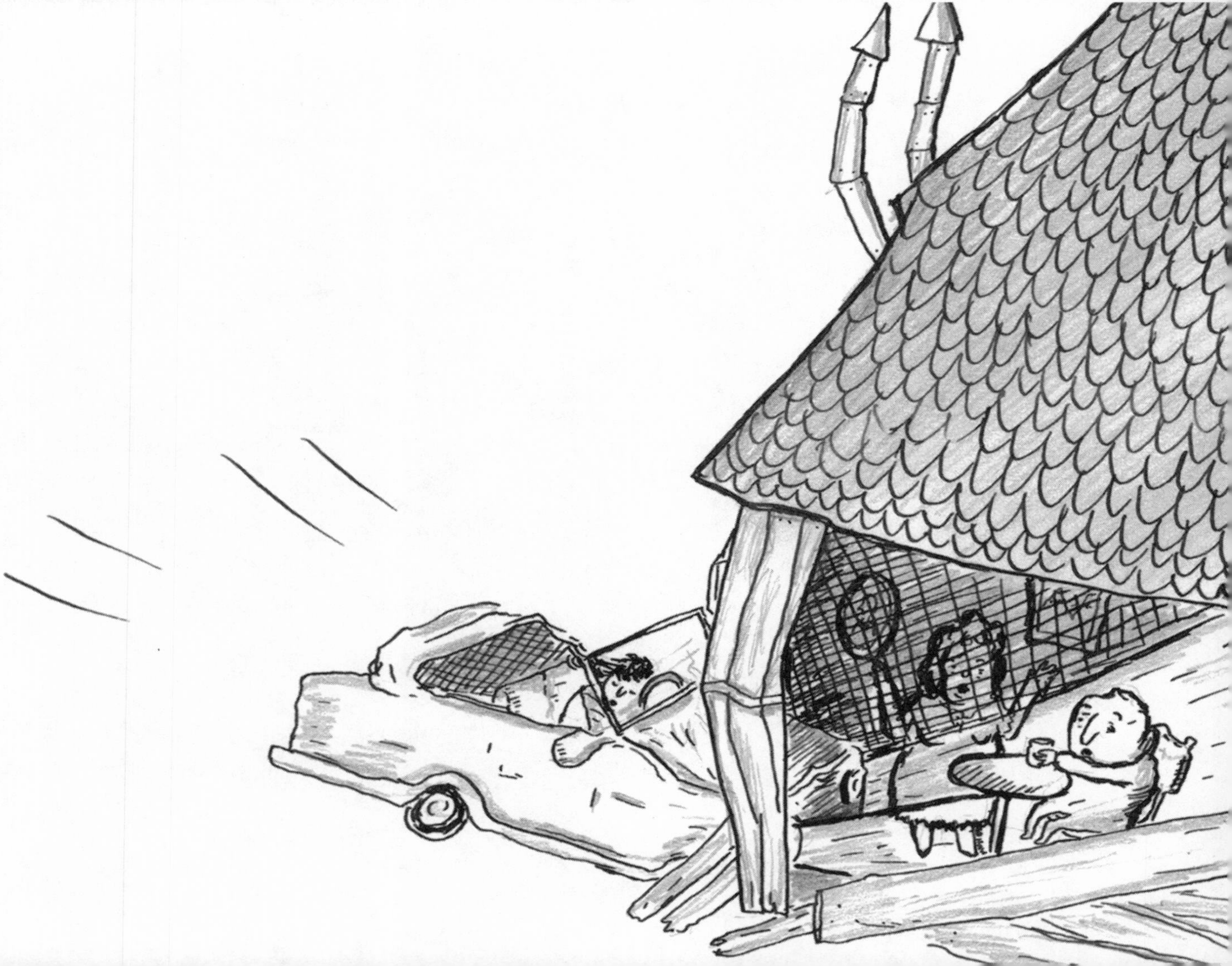

When I regained consciousness, I was lying in a bed in a dusty room. I looked around to find some sort of clue to where I was—FOOTSTEPS. No time. WHERE WAS MY GUN?

I scrambled. Opened every cabinet and drawer. I rushed over to the side table.

AHA! My familiar friend! Griselda, my pistol from Argentina.

As the footsteps got closer, I held my gun in my foot, ready . . .

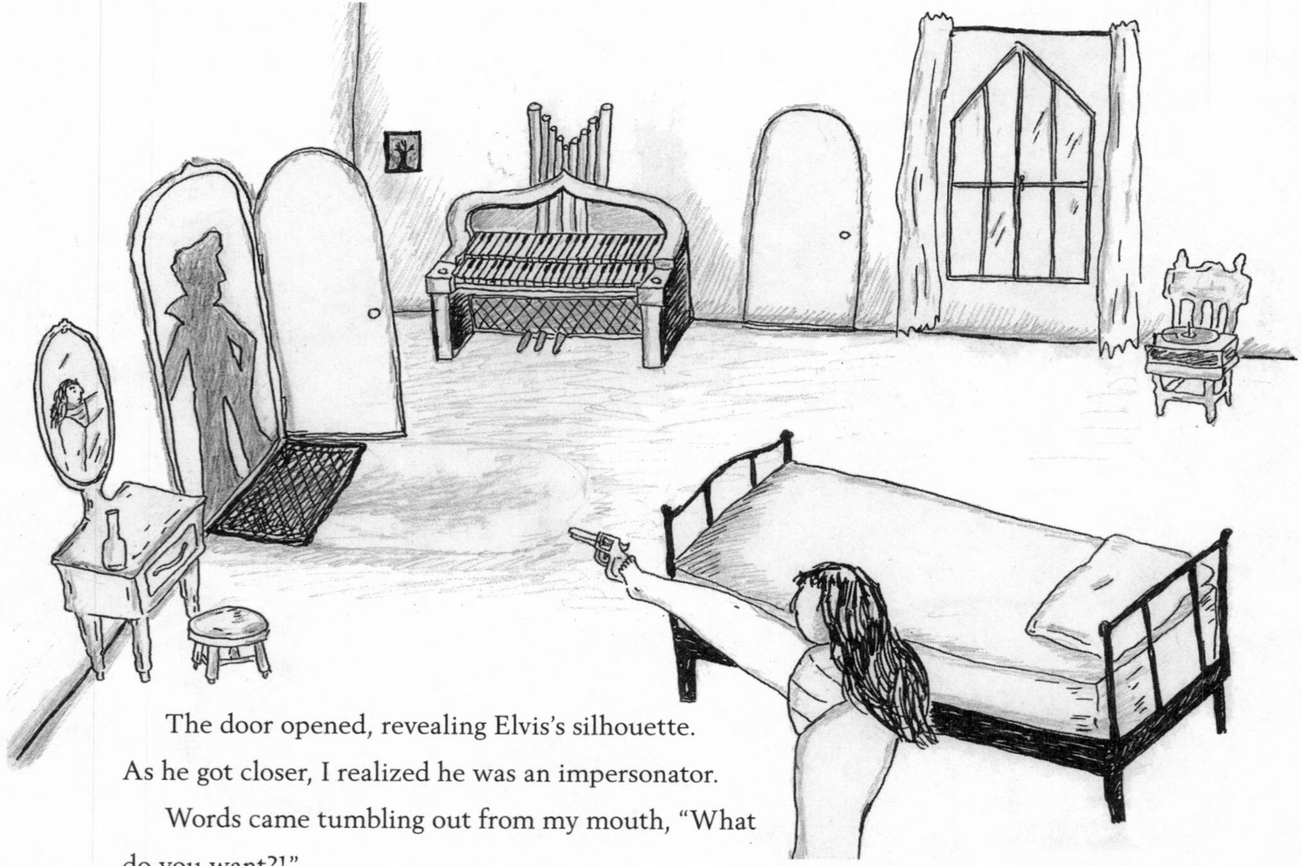

The door opened, revealing Elvis's silhouette. As he got closer, I realized he was an impersonator.

Words came tumbling out from my mouth, "What do you want?!"

"Nothing. I just want to help."

Could I trust him? I stood still. He didn't. He continued to get closer and for some reason I cocked the gun. My head felt strange. And then, everything went black.

I felt arms holding me, then darkness swallowed me whole.
Chills ran all over my body . . . and a wet towel laid on my forehead.

"You have a fever."

I looked around and saw an Elvis impersonator.

"I'm Cassady."

"Agatha."

"Where were you headed before you crashed into our building?"

"I'm off on a mission."

"Oh . . ." he stared. "To find God?"

"No. The Devil. I'm going to kill him."

I could see this resonate with him as he stoically nodded.

"I too have some unfinished business with that demon."

"We all do."

I squinted as if that would help me see what kind of person he is. He squinted back.

"You need to take me with you . . ."

THE SILVER MOON BEAMED A SPOTLIGHT ONTO CASSADY

Around the time of the first big heat wave, I confessed my love to sweet Lily. We decided to run away together and get married. Thought it would be funny to do an Elvis-themed wedding. Little did I know I would be wearing this suit for the rest of my life . . .

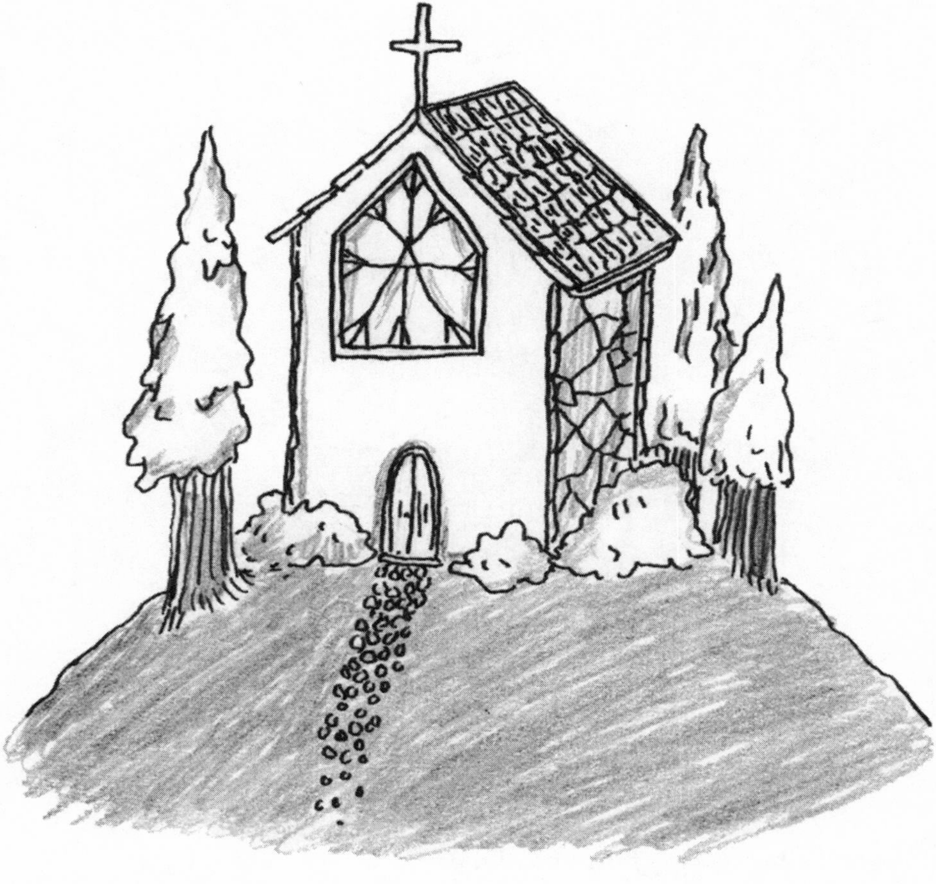

My love, Lily, walked down the aisle, while just outside the church was the beginning of the end of the world.

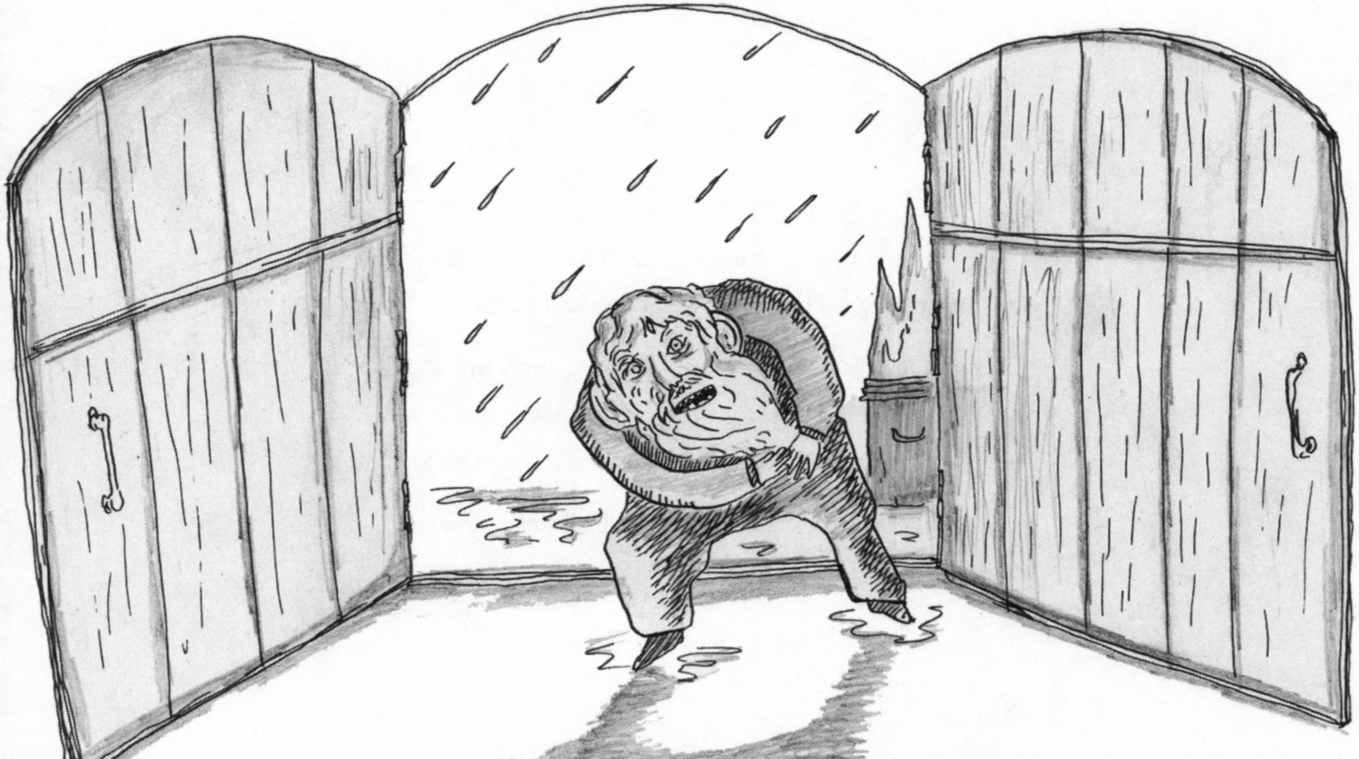

In the midst of our vows the doors broke open, and in splurged a wild-eyed man.

The man yelled gibberish at us. I assumed he wanted money and offered what we had to him.

The fever was severe. He started to bark at us in tongues. We tried our best to communicate but it was no use, he was no longer himself but a demon instead.

He pulled out his pistol, pointed it at me, and pulled the trigger.

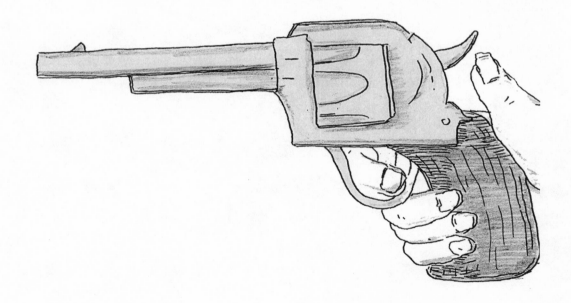

Lily, a fool, saved my life by ending hers.

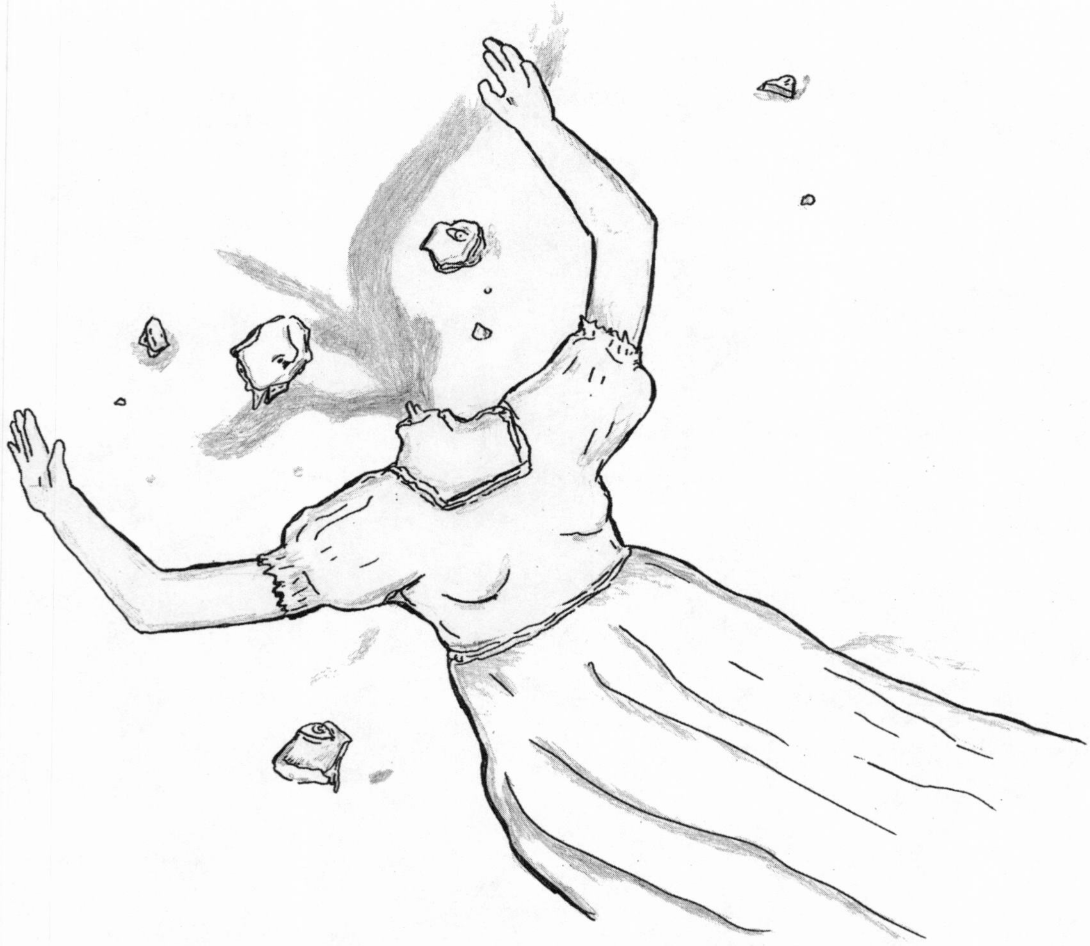

Her beautiful face, broken like a puzzle.
I kept trying to put her back together. But I
couldn't.

The Devil came and claimed her as his. Said
it was self-sacrifice. Suicide. Who knew saving
someone's life was a sin?

It's funny, the one thing Lily tried to pre-
vent happening happened. That night I died.
I don't know if I believe in God, but I sure as
hell believe in the Devil.

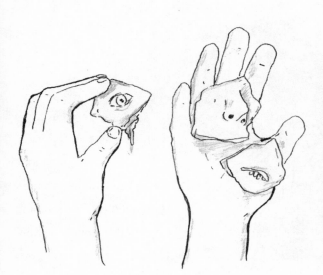

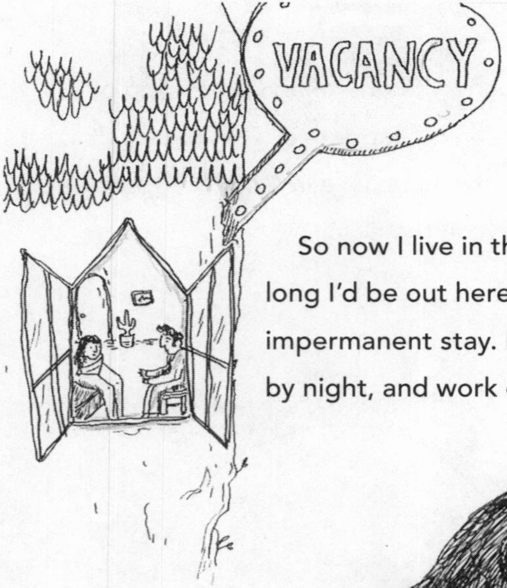
VACANCY

So now I live in this motel. I never knew how long I'd be out here, so I am permanently on an impermanent stay. I sing at the lounge as Elvis by night, and work on this organ by day.

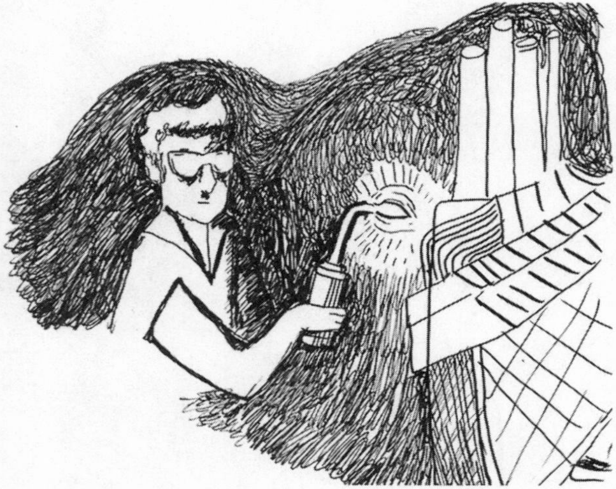

Cassady stared at me with weight. I stared back at him. He stood up and walked toward a trunk in the corner of his room and opened it. "I want to show you something."

The room began to fill with an awful smell. I couldn't tell what he was pulling out . . . it looked like a sewn doll . . . and then . . . I pieced it together. He was holding—

"This is my ex-wife, Lily."

"Jesus Christ."

"I built this organ. When I hook her body up to it, the sound waves make her body move again."

He began to play the keys and Lily's body started slowly dancing. "The only thing is, when she actually gets moving, she's still just an empty vessel. A dud-eyed zombie."

Cassady stopped playing and Lily's body began to lose its balance. Cassady caught her. He looked at her lovingly, "She needs her soul to be complete and the Devil has it. That's why you need to take me with you to Hell. We can fight side by side."

"You know . . . you could've just asked. You didn't have to make your ex-wife's corpse do a song and dance for me . . . You're even crazier than I thought. Let's go."

I looked out the window, saw my convertible, and jumped.

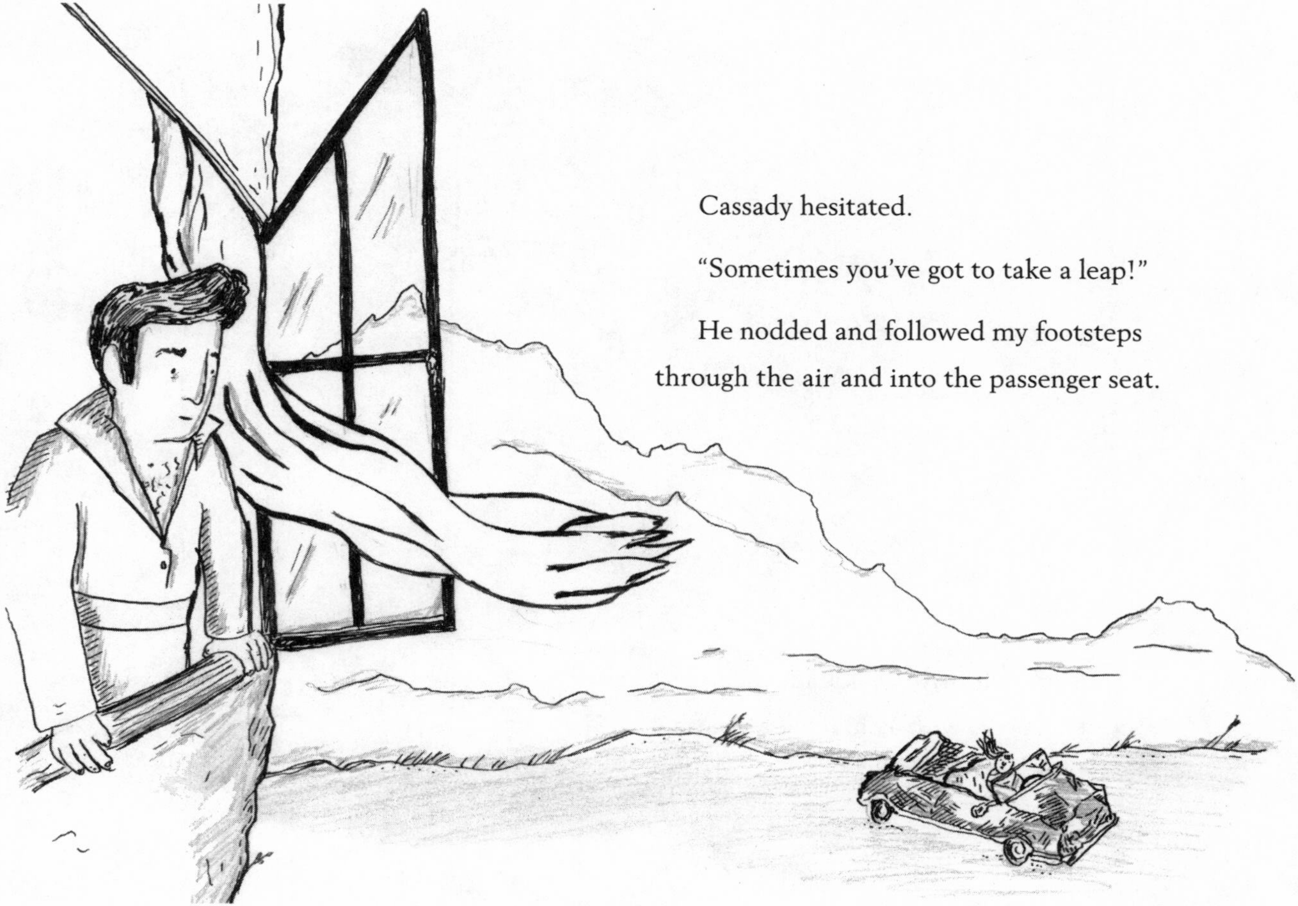

Cassady hesitated.

"Sometimes you've got to take a leap!"

He nodded and followed my footsteps through the air and into the passenger seat.

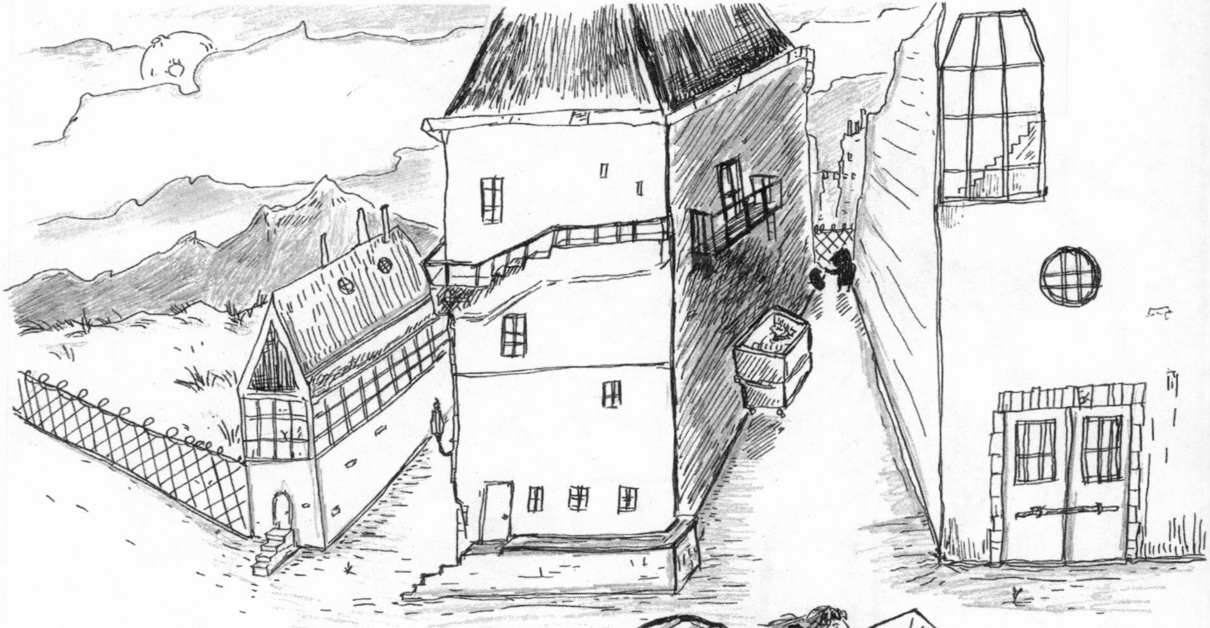

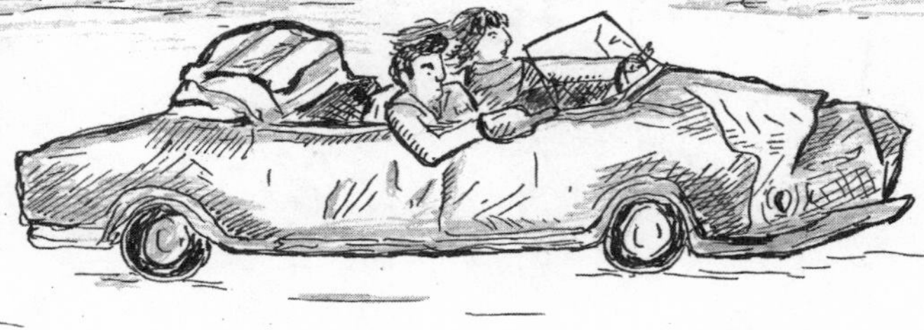

Along our drive we found ourselves crossing paths with a child whose mother had succumbed to the fever. Cassady and I pulled over.

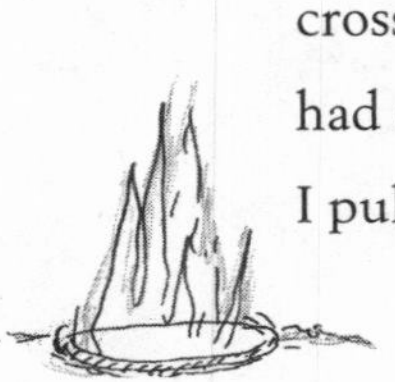

We walked down the alley and made a vow to defend the world together. Cassady winked at me, curled into a stepping plateau, and I took that extra step to kick that mother right in the face!

A man watching from the fire escape yelled, "Damn, she's all legs!"

I turned to the man and looked him in the eye, "Damn straight."

Cassady smiled at me, but it was soon washed away when a shadow loomed over us. When we turned around we were face-to-face with a large Russian man. His arms lunged for us, I tried to dodge them but it was no use, he lifted us both and let out a big belly laugh.

He yelled, "THANK YOU SO MUCH FOR KICK-ING WIFE IN FACE AND SAVING OUR CHILD!! I am Natchesky!" He was red with joy. "Come follow us." He took his little girl's hand.

"We live underground where it's safe. We will show you good time. Celebrate with me life—for my child is alive! And BONUS, I have lived long enough to see wife get kicked in face!"

He handed us a beer and introduced us to his village, each time retelling his favorite story of how I kicked his wife in the face. We celebrated all night, but our victory was yet to be had.

I couldn't sleep, so I sat at the end of the road and let my feet dangle. I heard footsteps. I turned—it was Cassady.

Cassady stared at me with his heart, "Wild night, huh?" I nodded and took a swig of my beer. His lips broke apart, "Have you ever lost anyone?"

"When I was really young . . . I remember being at my grandfather's funeral. You know that game when you're a kid where you jump from one thing to another and pretend the ground is lava?"

Cassady nodded.

"Well, I remember jumping from one gravestone to another, trying not to fall onto the grass. I didn't realize how disrespectful it was. I didn't realize what was underneath those stones. I remember seeing my grandfather's body in the open casket later that morning, but I couldn't absorb that that was actually him. It didn't look like him. A soulless body isn't the same person . . . And with all that they do to their bodies to prepare them for the viewing . . . The word 'death' had no meaning until months later . . ."

I tried to stop myself from crying, but I couldn't. So Cassady held me, and I cried anyway. "I'm so dumb, Cassady. I was staring right at his face. It wasn't til almost six months after he died that I realized that was him . . . He was the only person I've ever loved."

Cassady picked me up, letting my face drip all over his shoulder, and carried me to the roof. He sang me a beautiful melody til my heart could rest again.

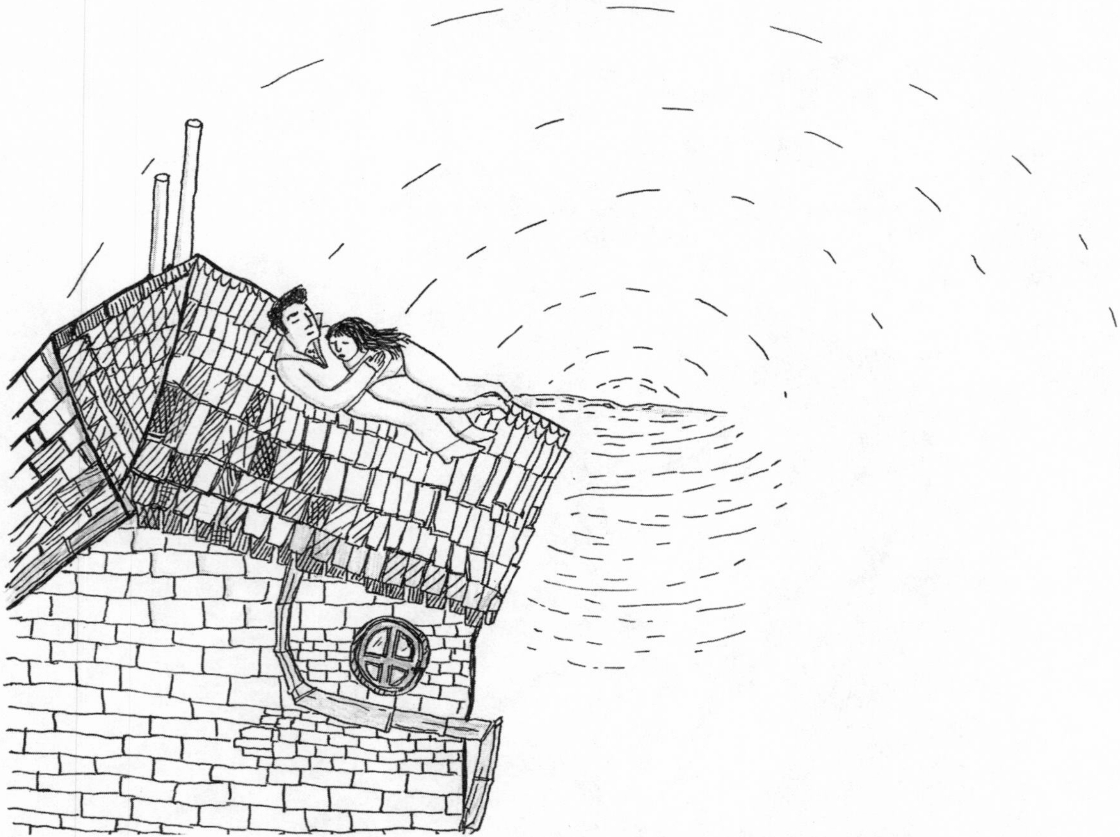

I could feel the shy, peeking light of the morning kiss me on my cheek. When I opened my eyes I was lying on Cassady's chest. He was glowing, illuminated by the sunrise. Embarrassed, we both smiled.

I got up and started to run toward my convertible. "Let's hit the road, shall we?"

Cassady nodded, "We'll race the sun."

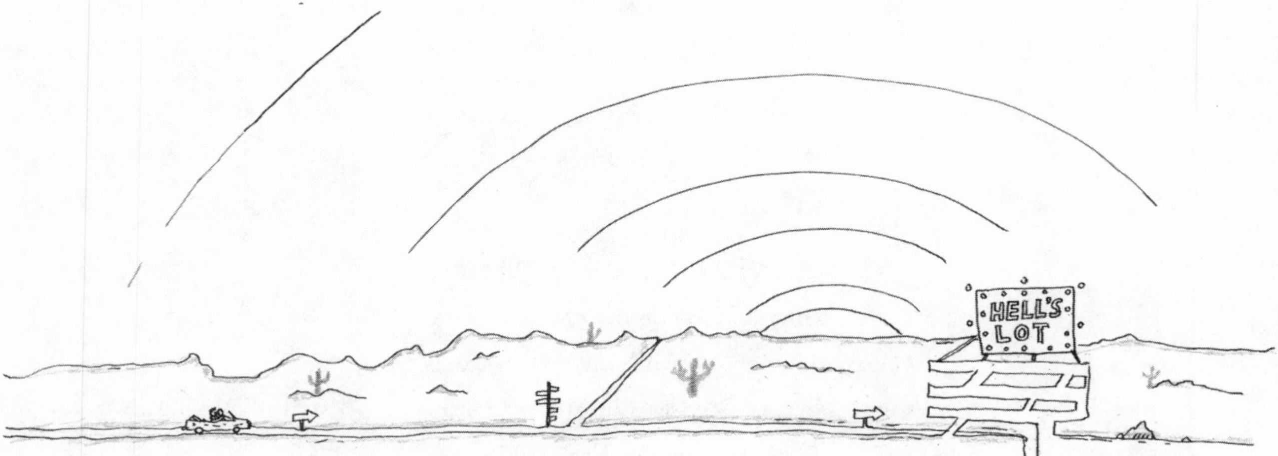
HELL'S
LOT

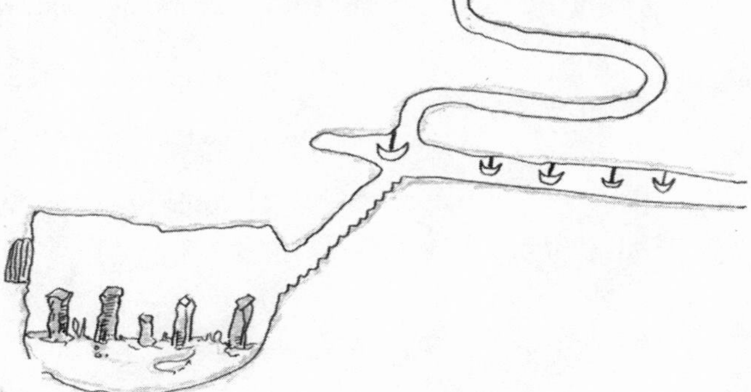

We followed all the "Hell" signs that lead us to its exact whereabouts. Hell was hidden at the bottom level of a parking structure.

We got out of the car and marched right up to those huge wooden doors. The doors cracked open, and darkness spilled all around us.

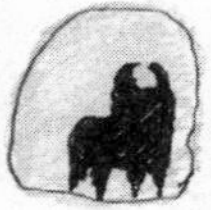

A gust of cold wind blew from the hall of howling souls. We stuck close, so we wouldn't get lost. And at the end of the hall we were confronted with a new challenge . . . a game of Hot Lava.

Cassady jumped first. I followed.

The Devil had been watching us the whole way, he was smiling.

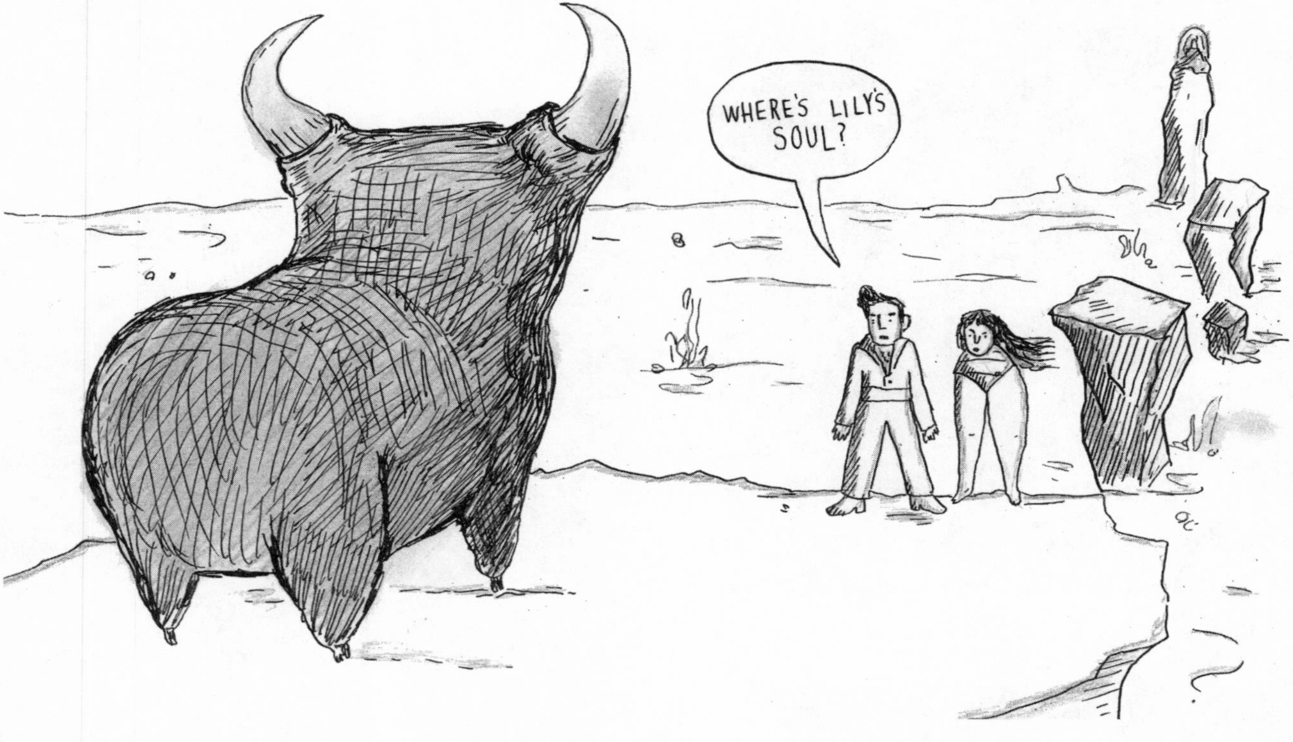
WHERE'S LILY'S SOUL?

Cassady lunged at the Devil with a dance, kicking the Devil's beady eyes. I climbed onto the Devil while he was down. I tried to wrestle the old cow by his horns, but he shook me right off, throwing me through the roof of Hell and into a sky abyss.

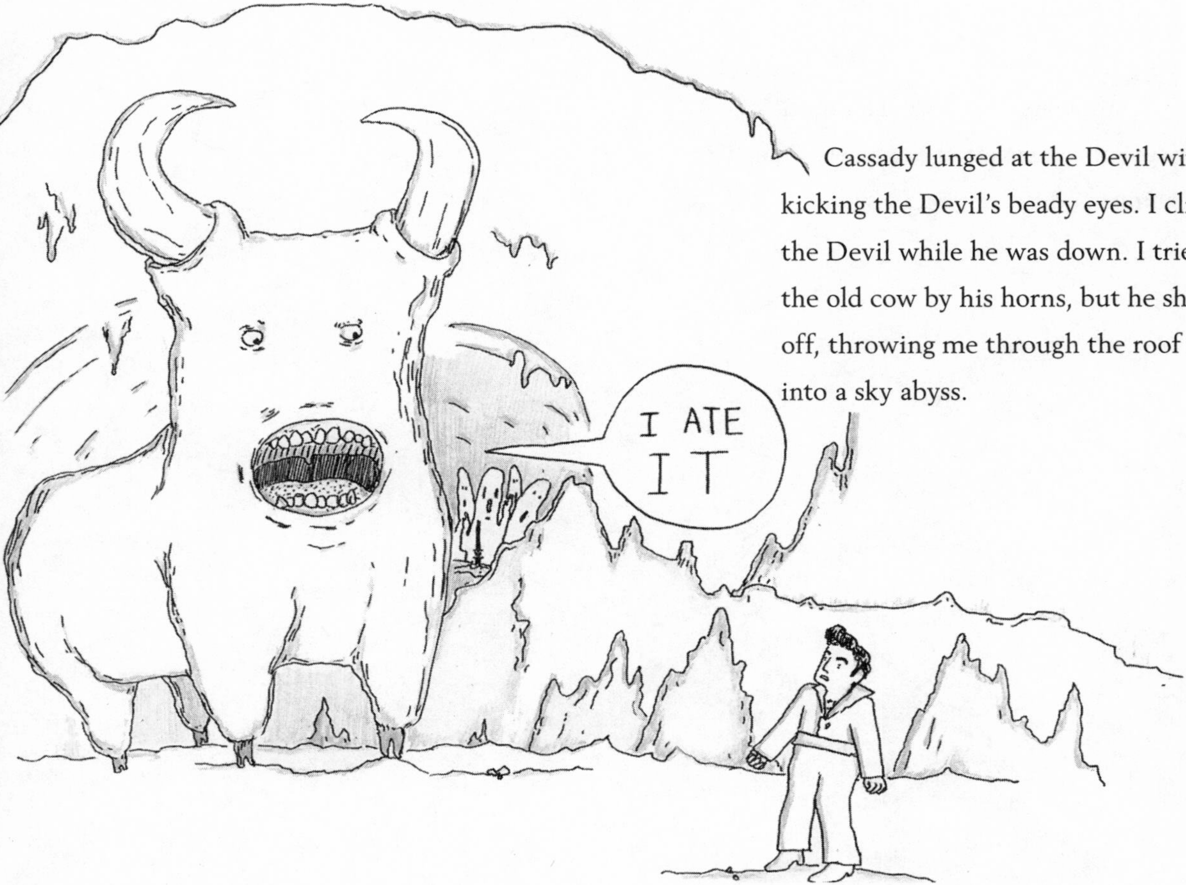
I ATE IT

I flew an unfathomable distance, landing all the way on the other side of the planet in the North Pole. That's where everything good is like Santa's Village.

I saw God.

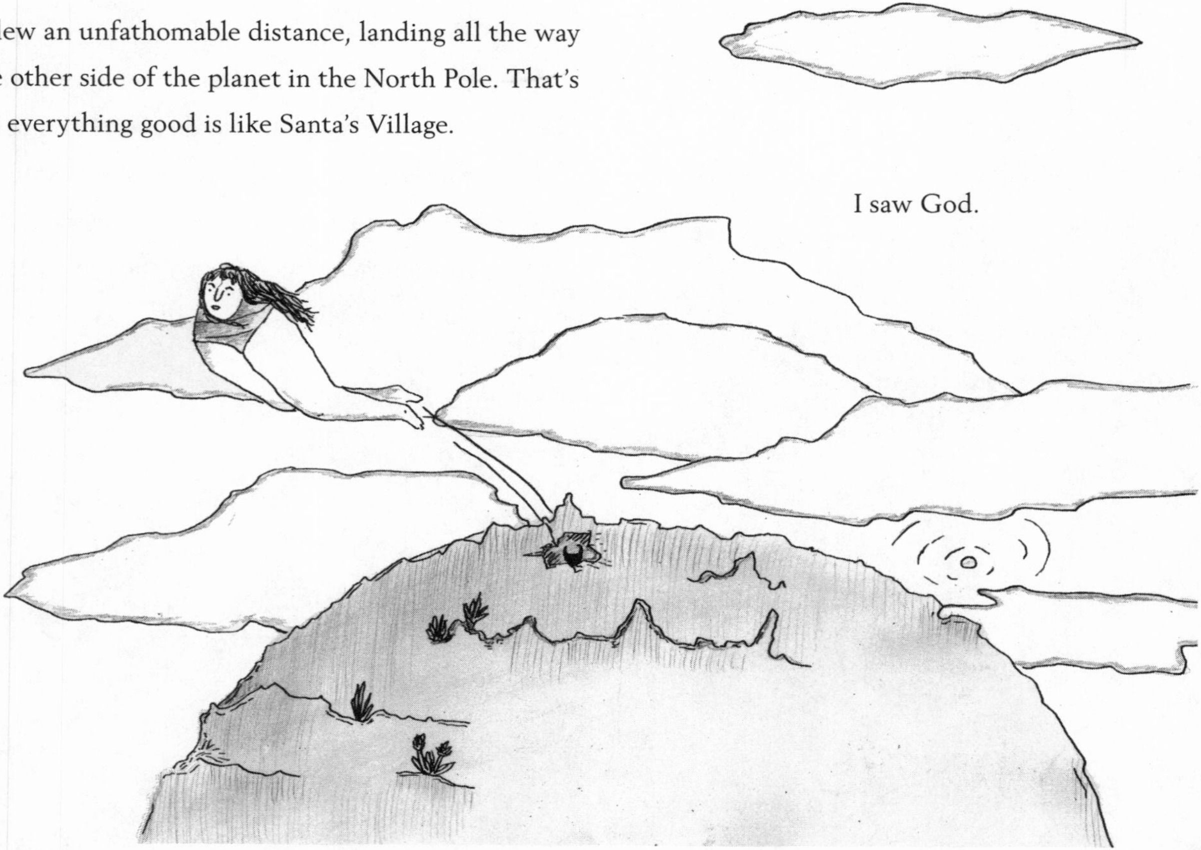

I asked Him, "Why aren't you helping? The world needs you."

"IT SEEMS LIKE YOU AND CASSADY
ARE DOING A PRETTY GOOD JOB
HANDLING IT YOURSELVES . . .
BESIDES, IMAGINE HOW
BORING LIFE WOULD BE
IF YOU DIDN'T HAVE POWER
OVER YOUR OWN DESTINY.
THIS IS YOUR ADVENTURE,
NOT MINE . . ."

I nodded, "Thank you." I started to walk back but remembered I was all the way at the North Pole. I had a long way to go. I turned to Him again, "God?"

"OF COURSE . . ."

He took my little body into a slingshot and
shot me back to the other side.

I screamed as I fell deeper and deeper into
the pits of Hell again.

Cassady recognized my voice and I fell right back into his arms again. "Are you trying to tell me something?"

For a moment I forgot the Devil was there.

The Devil roared, "I'M GOING TO EAT YOU LIKE A BANANA, SKIN PEELED FIRST!" He chased us.

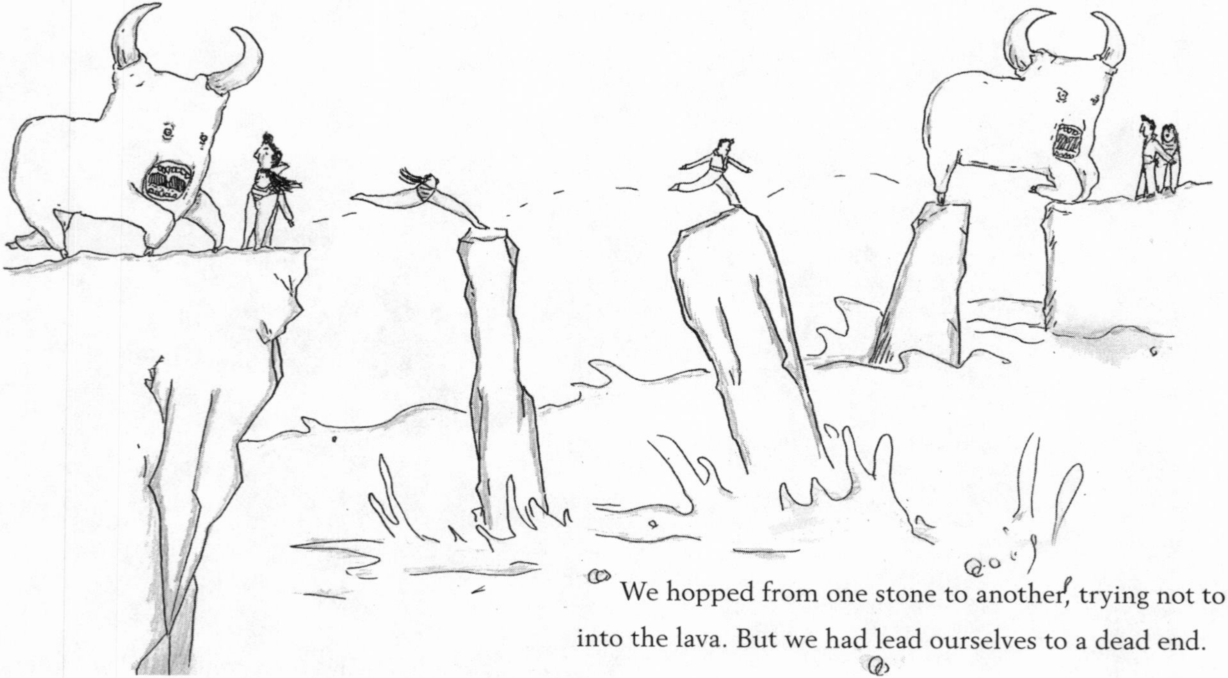

We hopped from one stone to another, trying not to fall into the lava. But we had lead ourselves to a dead end.

The Devil kicked dust into Cassady's eyes then stamped him in the gut. Cassady collapsed to his knees, he couldn't breathe, he started to curl into a ball.

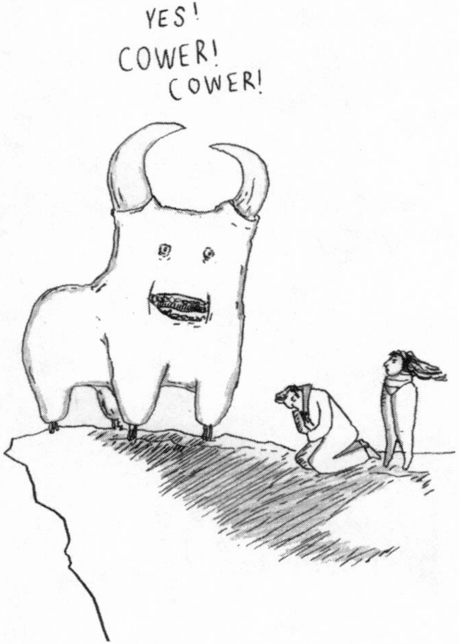
YES!
COWER!
COWER!

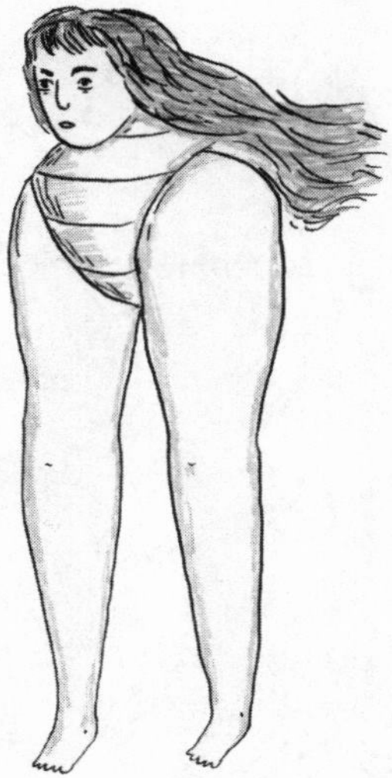

I couldn't take another disgusting second of this—so I took a leap and kicked that MOTHER right in the face.

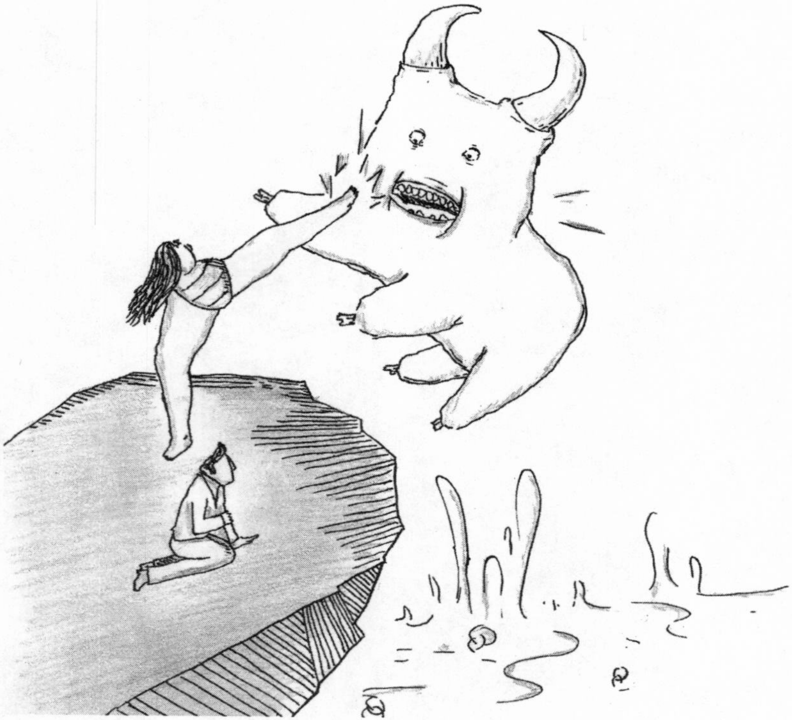

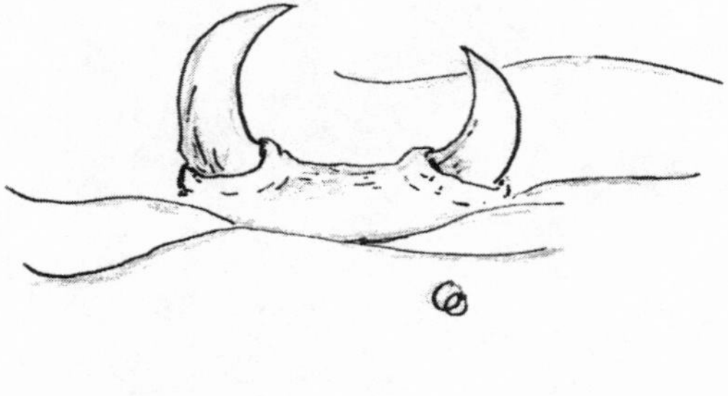

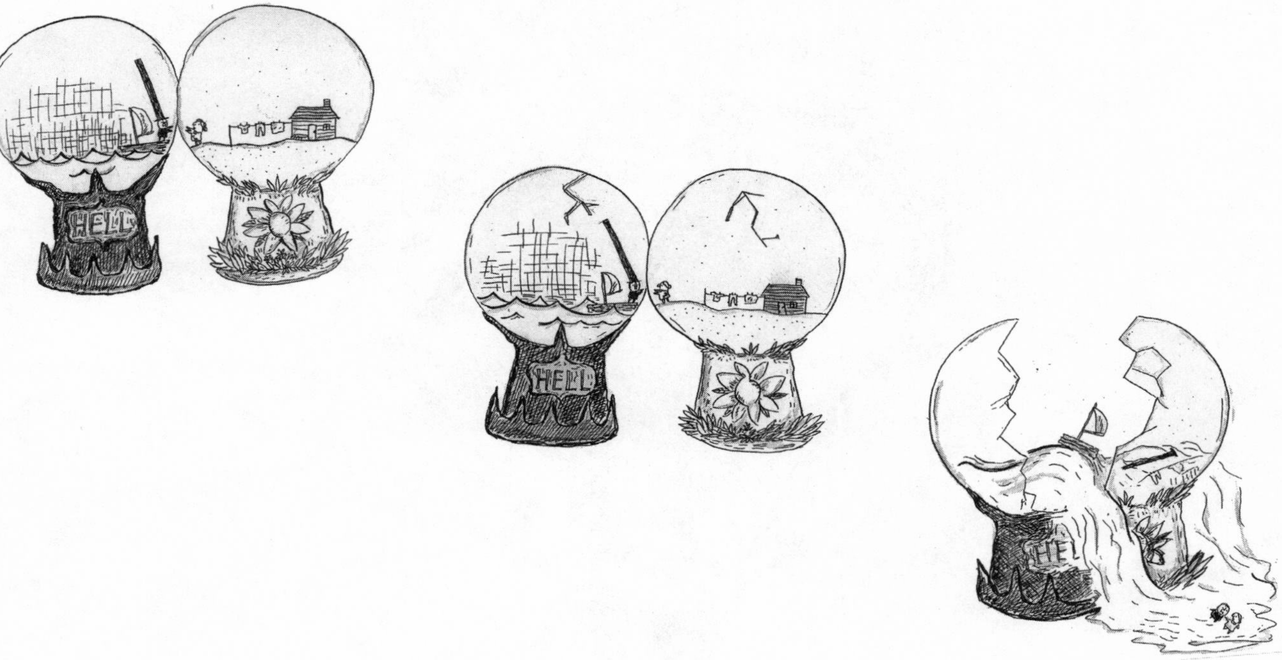
HELL
HELL
HEL

The pendulum of our hearts swung hard and fast. We had destroyed the Devil. We won. I felt our bodies getting closer.

I could feel his beautiful breath against my skin. We were alive. We had gotten exactly what we wanted . . . except . . .

A voice echoed in the distance yelling Cassady's name, and my heart sunk to the bottom of my gut.

It was Lily.

Cassady turned to catch her as she jumped and wrapped her arms around him. Something I could never do.

From the way he looked into her eyes I could tell he still loved her. Her soul was glowing like a billion golden dust particles in the sun. She was beautiful.

They spoke to each other in low voices. I couldn't make out the words. Cassady slowly made his way over to me.

He looked at me with weight in his eyes and said, "I was a widower when we met."

"I know." I wanted to pretend I didn't understand.

"Maybe we'll meet in another life."

"I look forward to that."

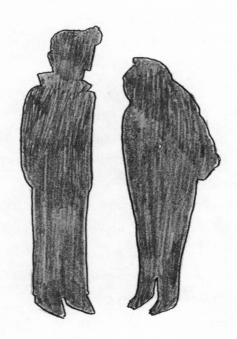

Cassady nodded, then
climbed out of Hell with his beloved Lily.

The end.

Love is a living, breathing thing.

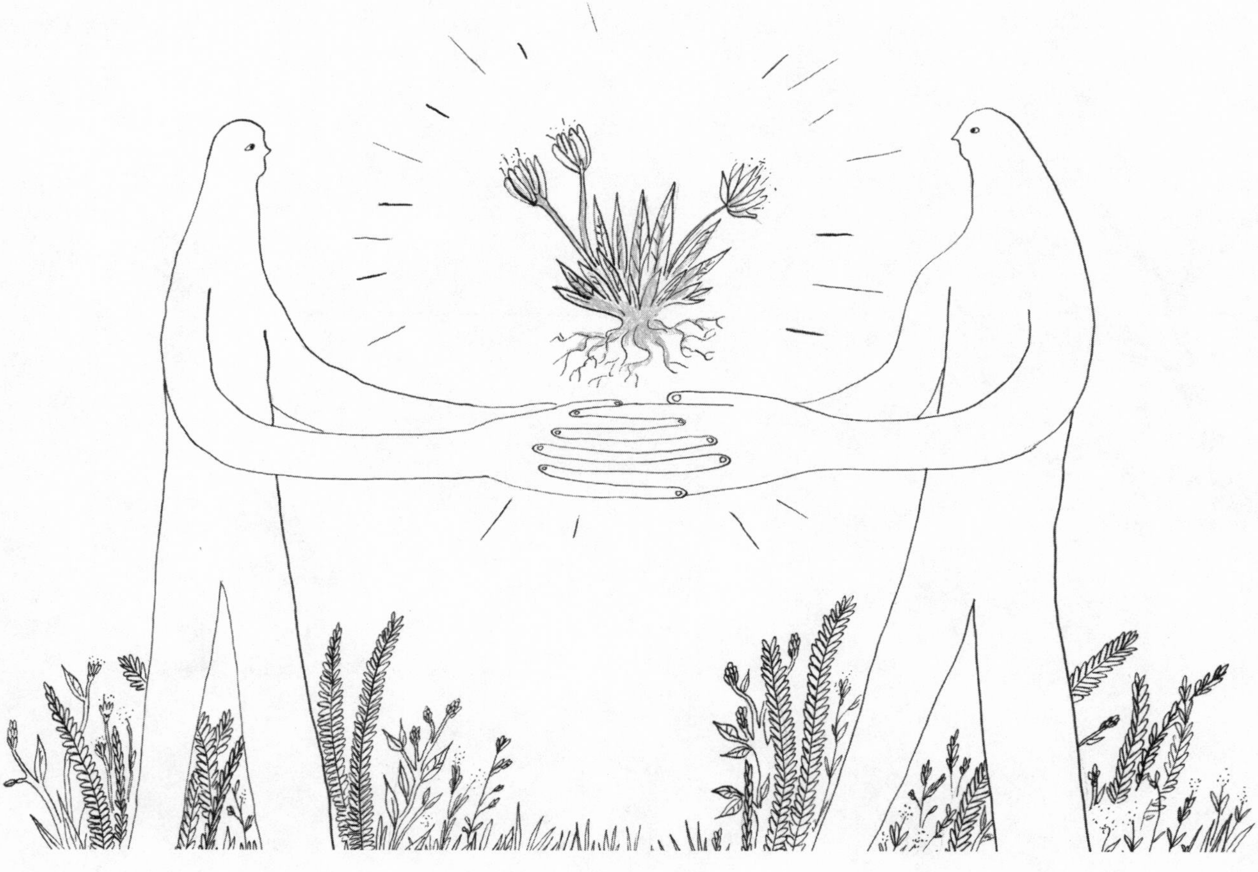

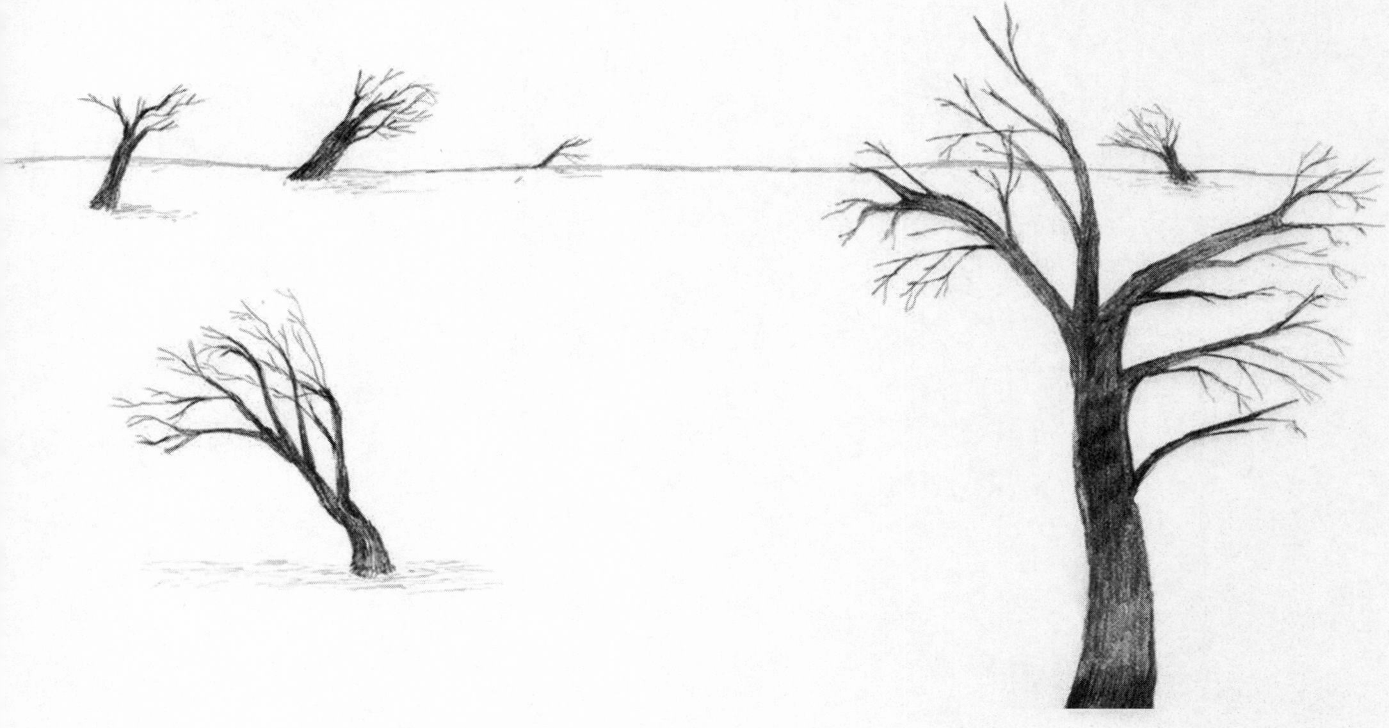

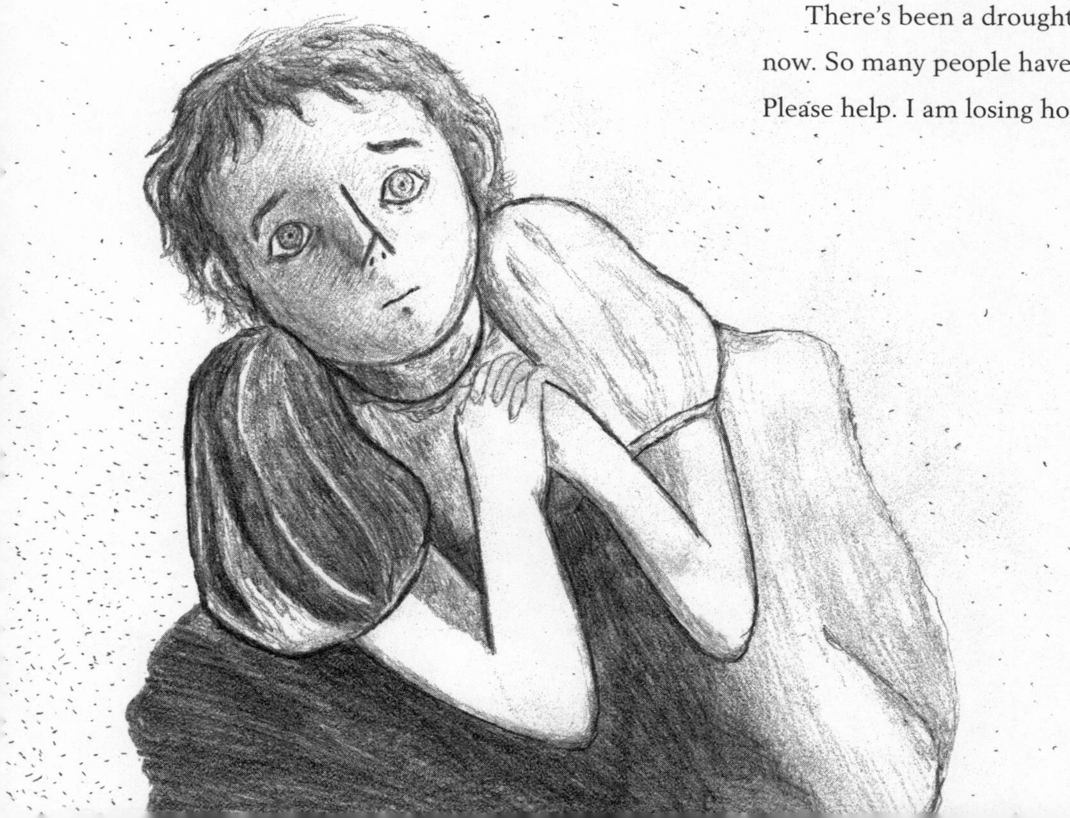

"I never learned how to pray . . . but I hope this works . . .

There's been a drought for over a decade now. So many people have died, and keep dying. Please help. I am losing hope."

THE CRESCENDO

Many battles have happened throughout the
span of time. And many lives were lost.

Those who could not continue on burst into a
billion molecules and floated back into the sky,
turning into clouds.

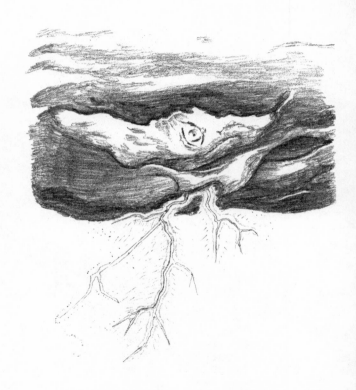

To follow through with the cloud cycle, they would need to precipitate.

Fearful of disappearing, they held on to themselves and refused to rain. But the more they held on to their grief, the heavier and darker their hearts got. And soon, the living things of Earth began to fall.

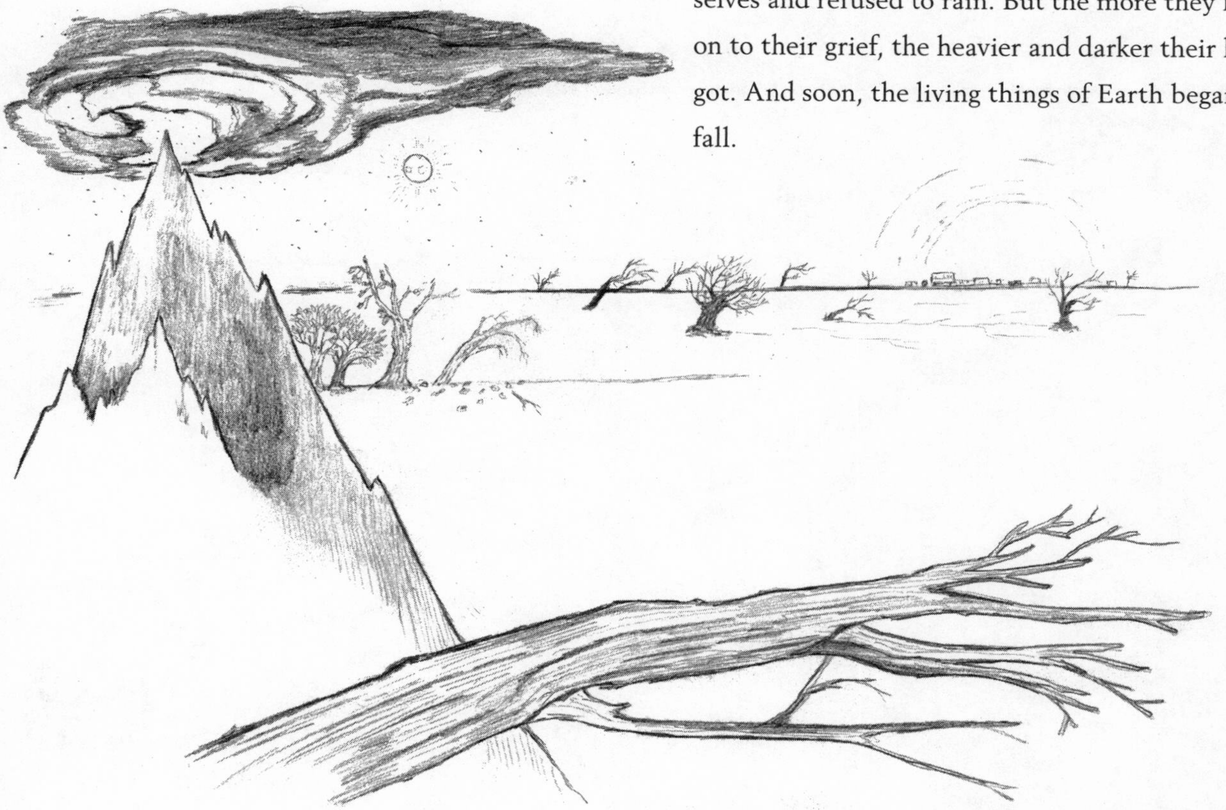

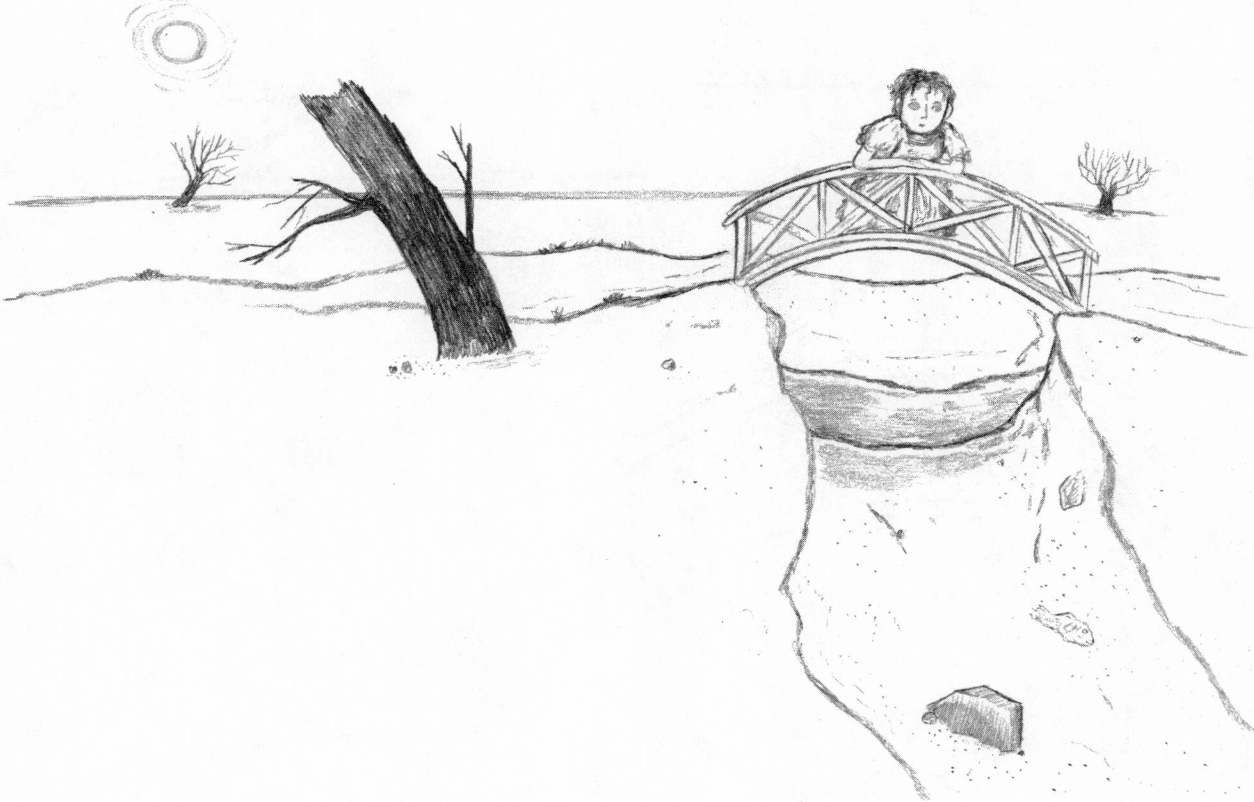

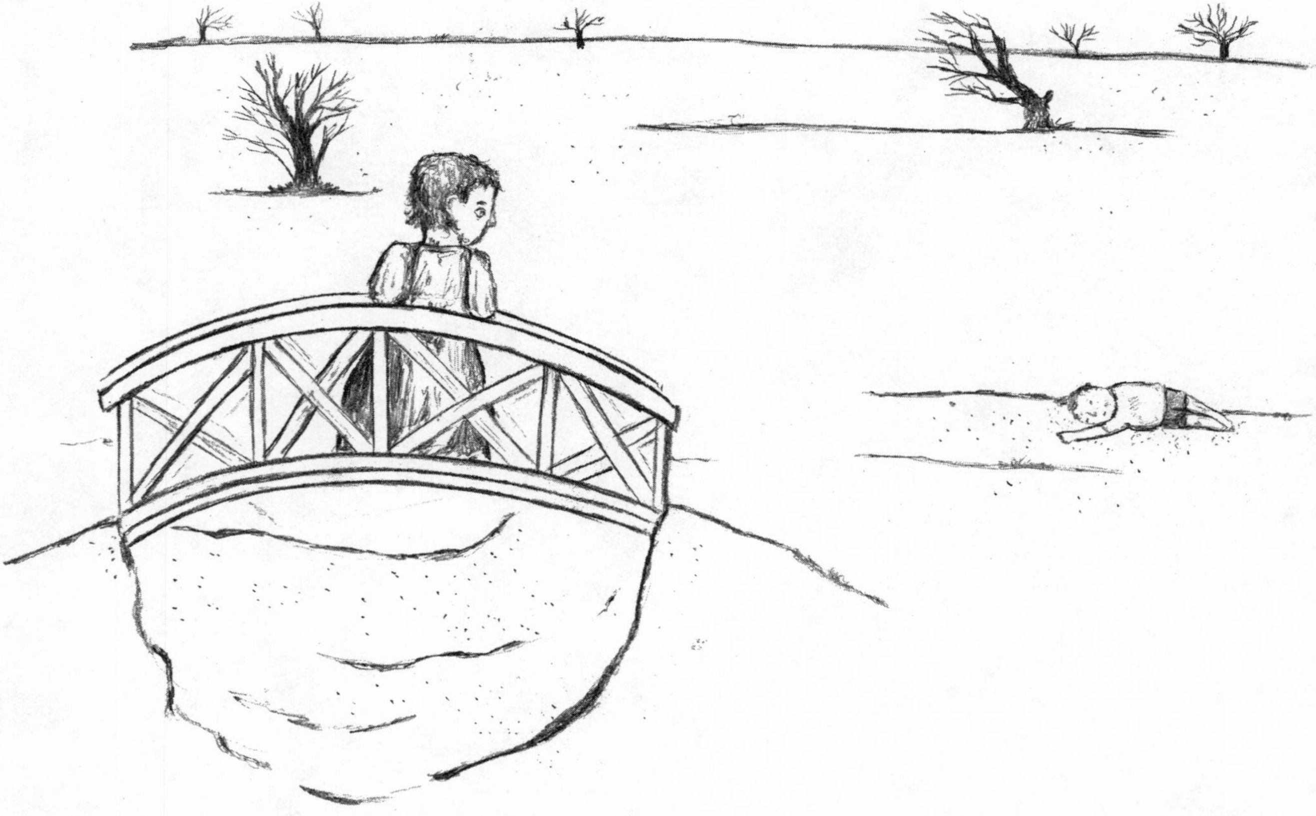

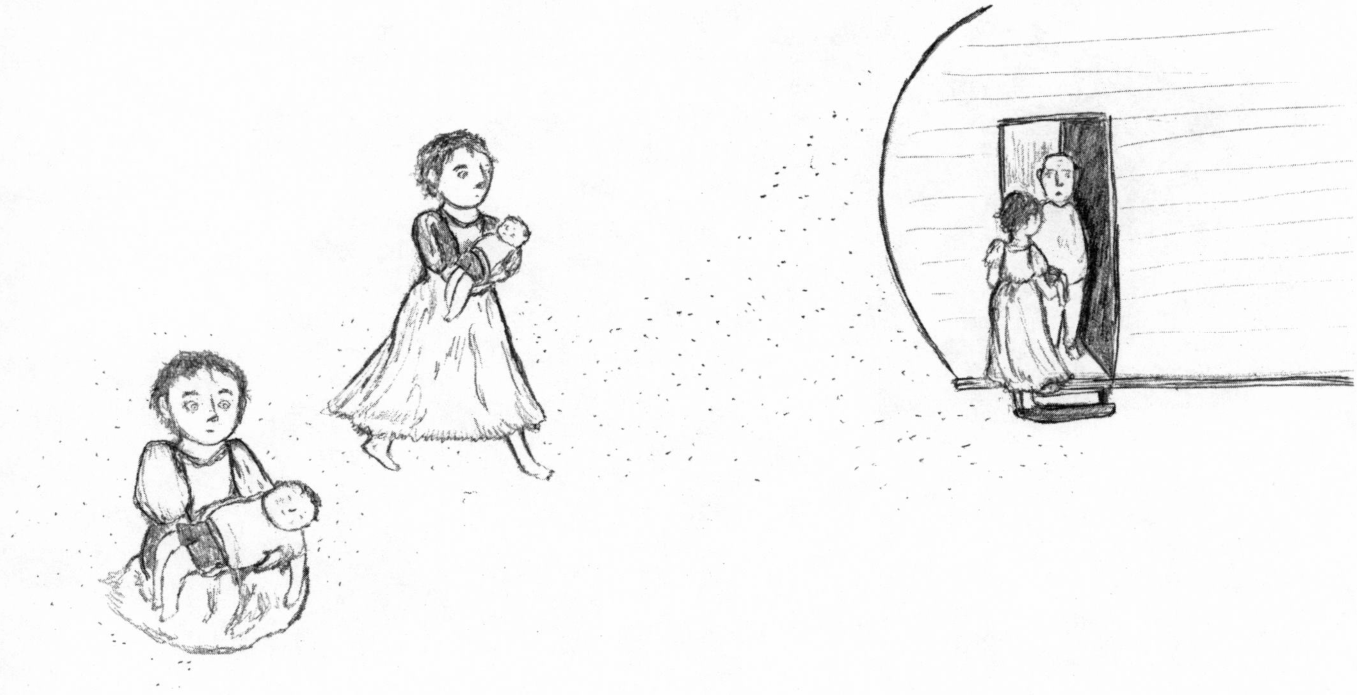

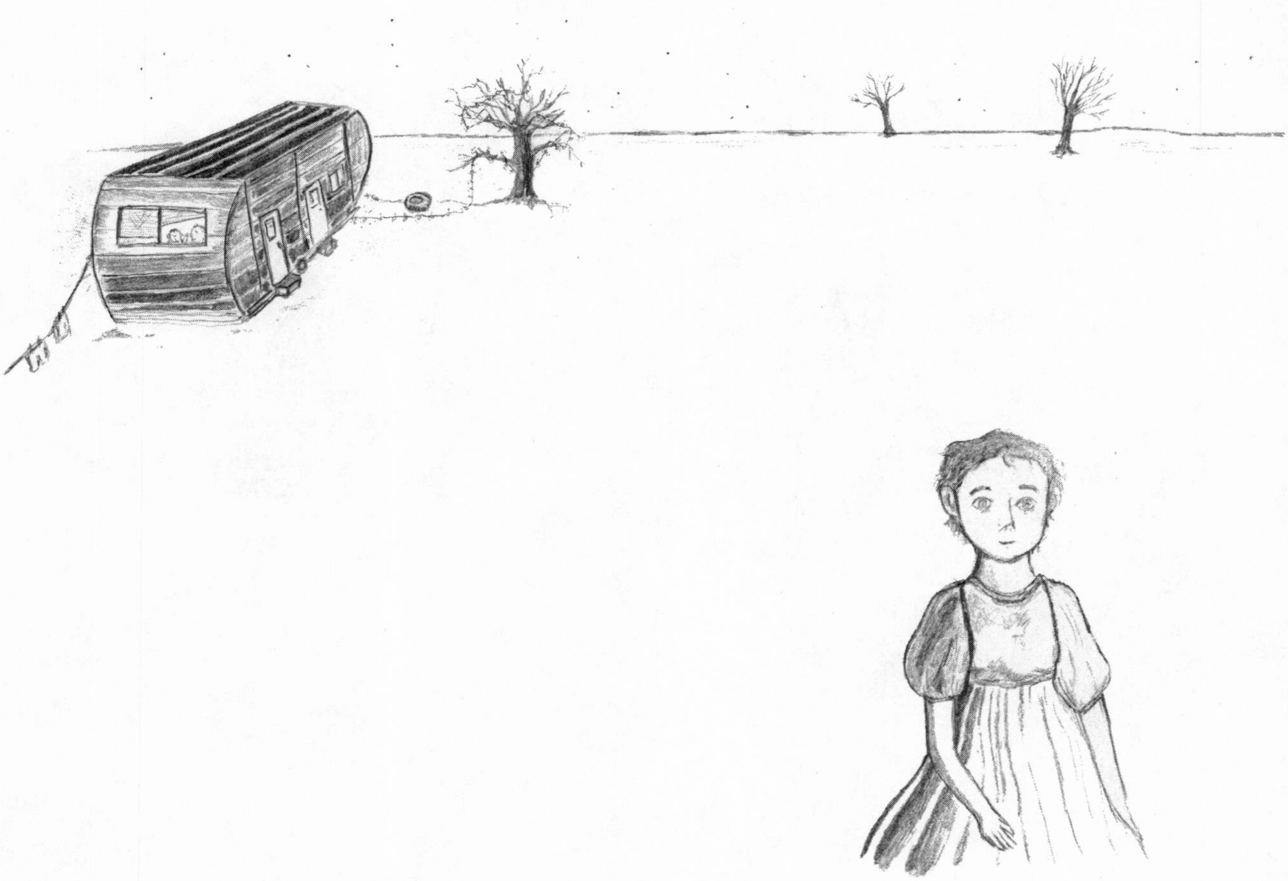

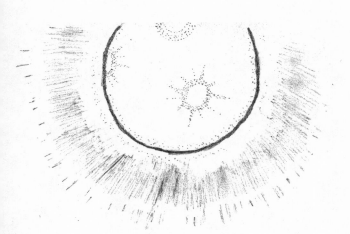

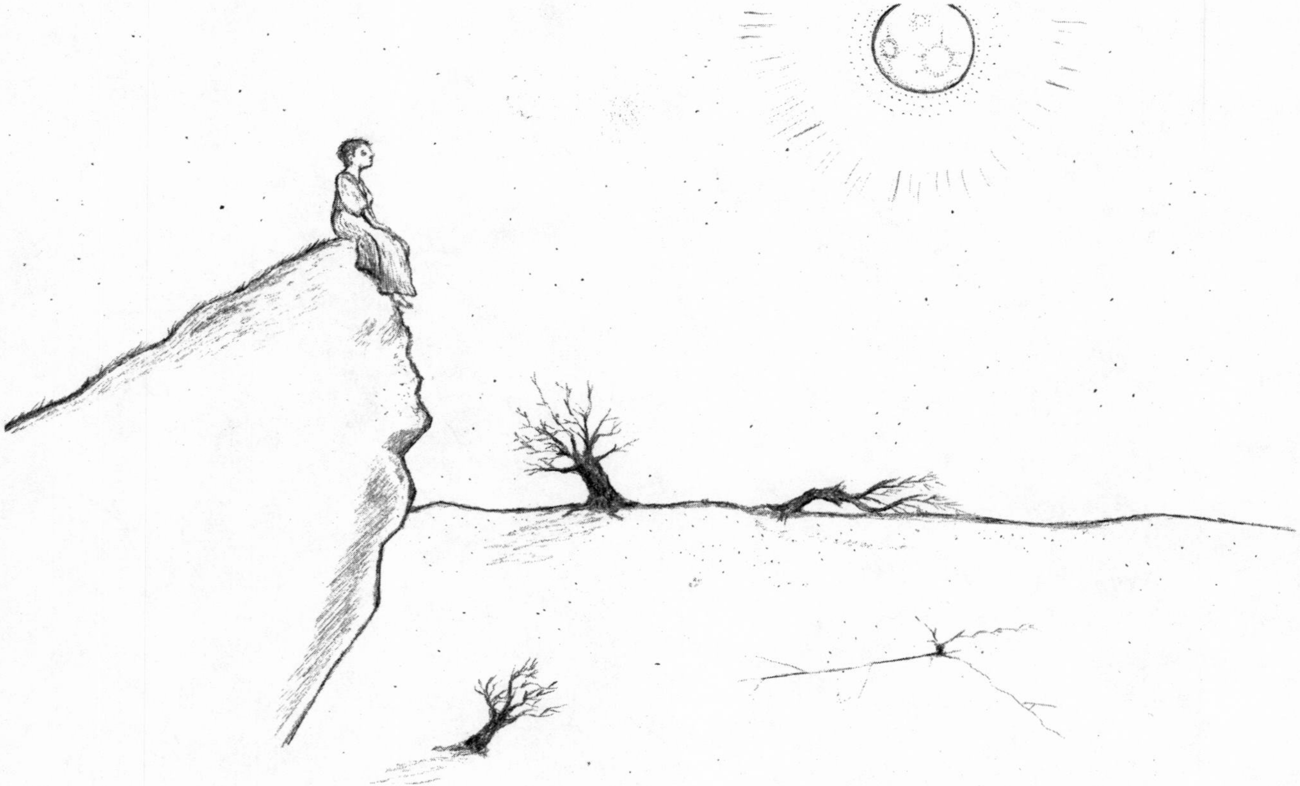

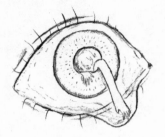

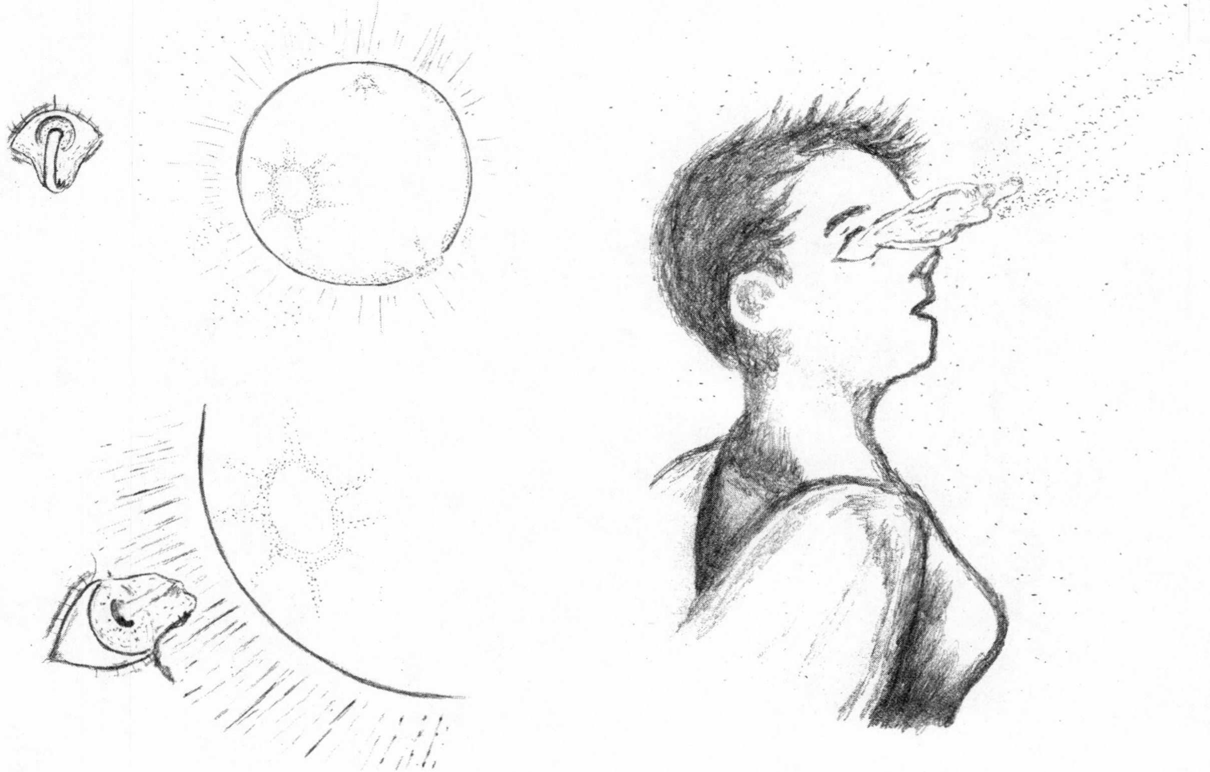

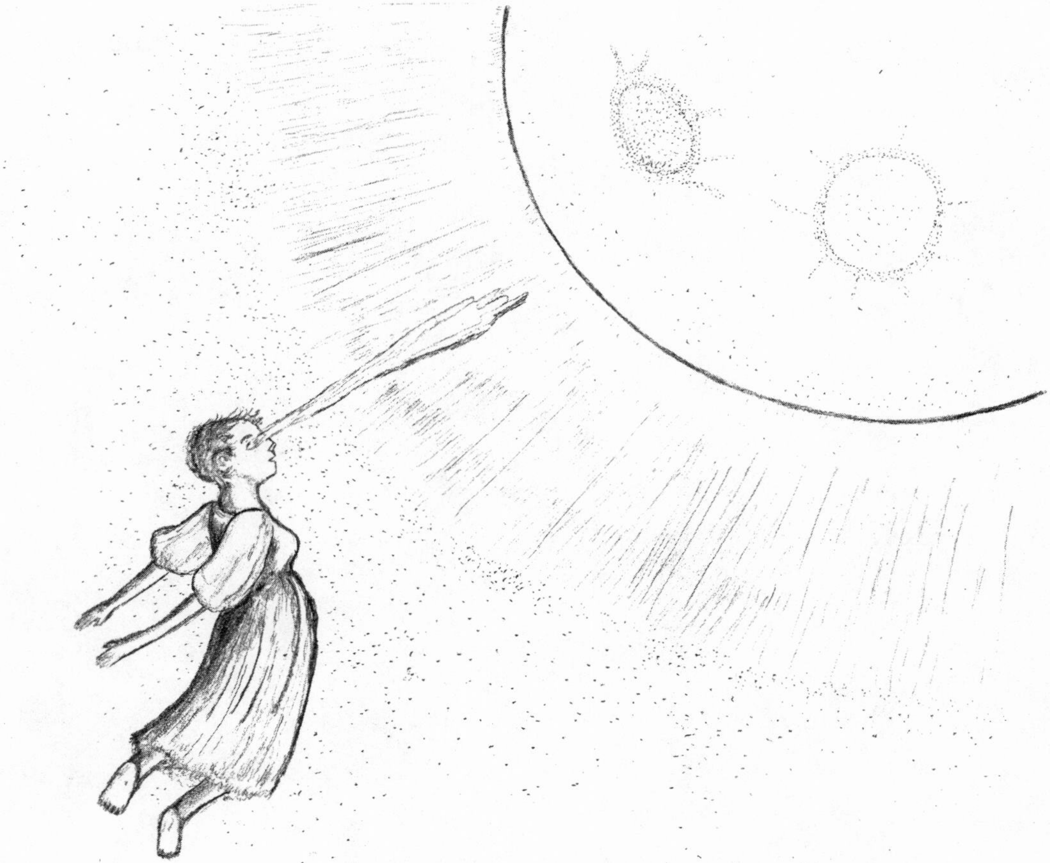

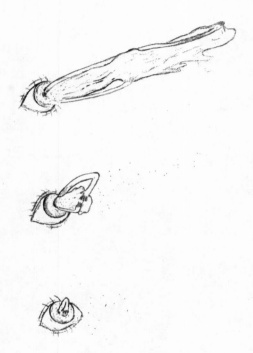

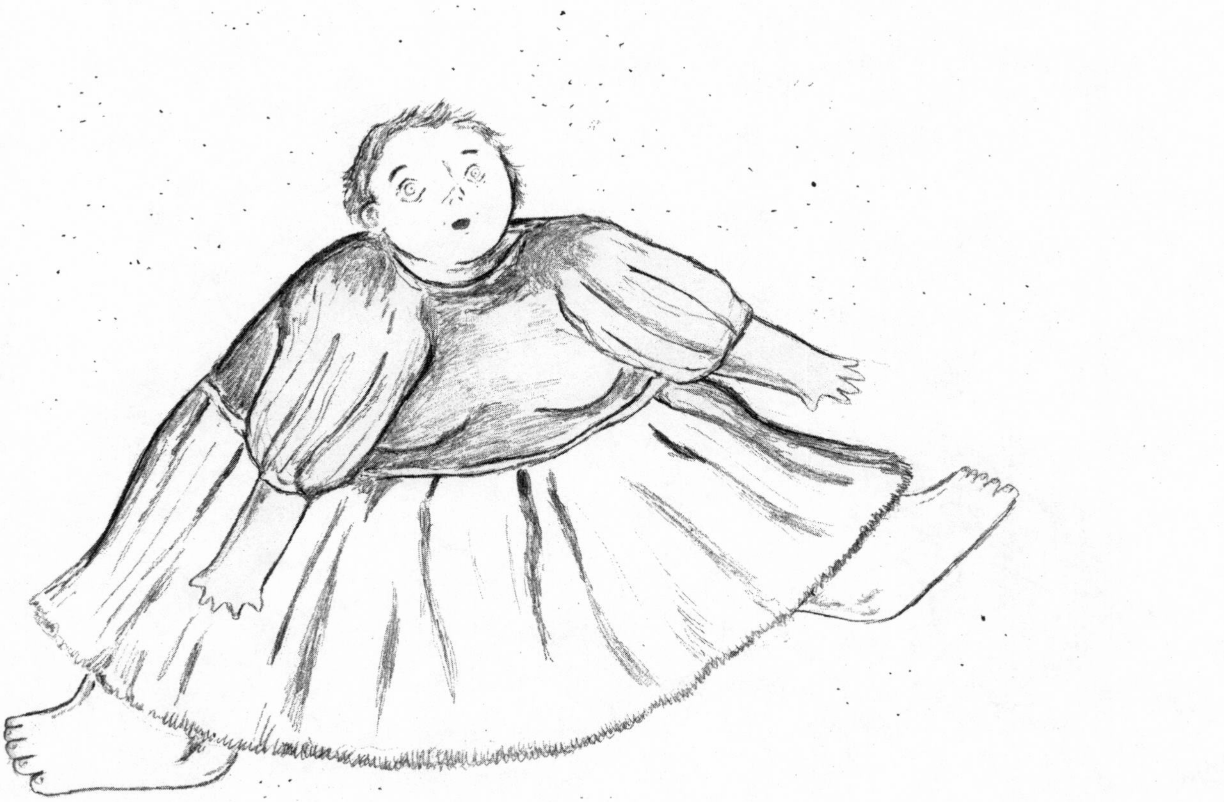

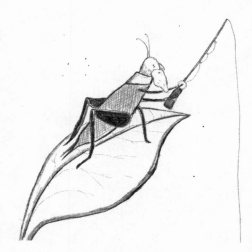

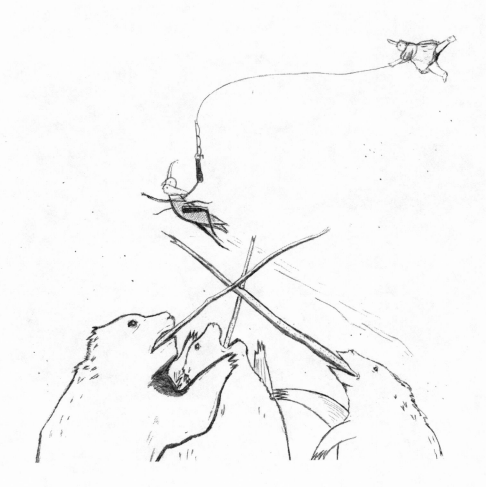

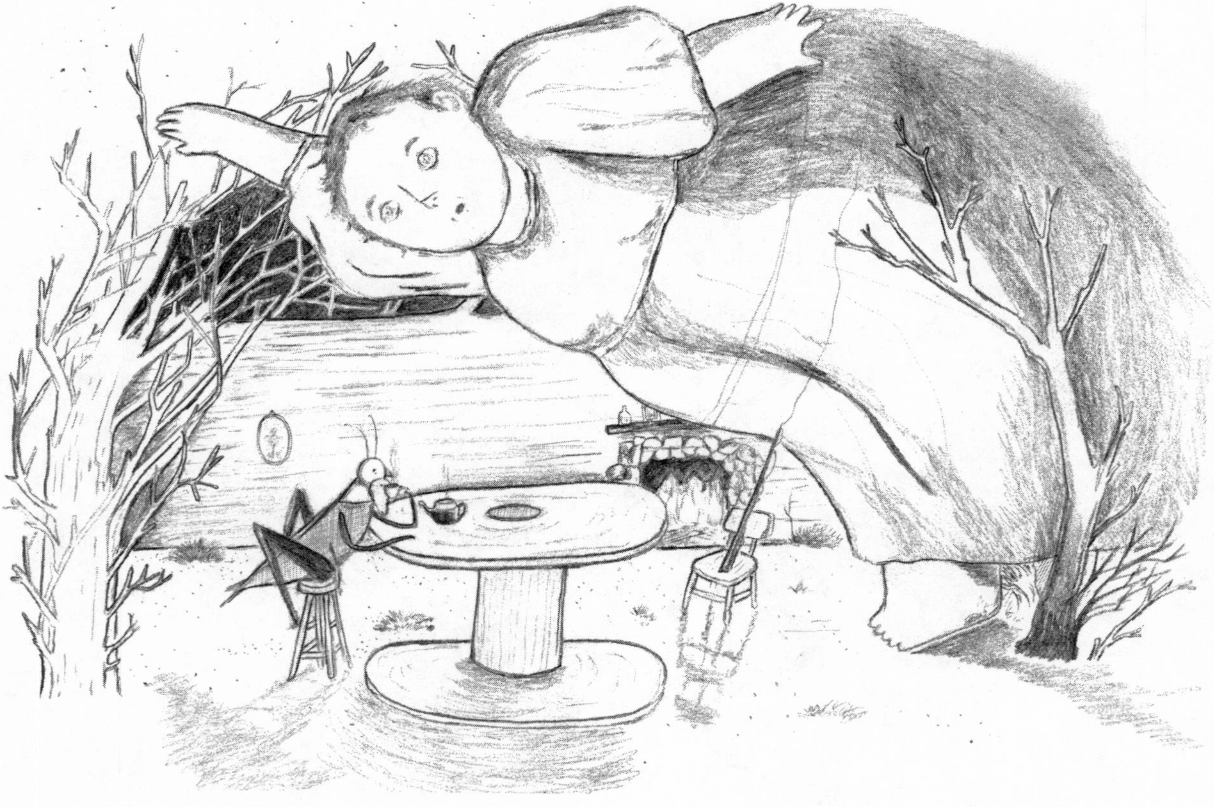

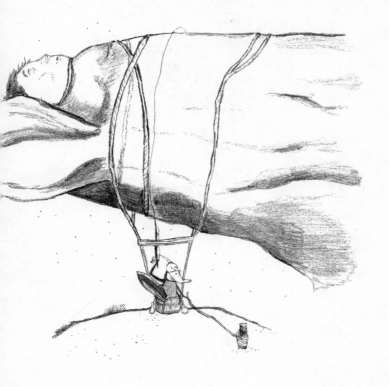

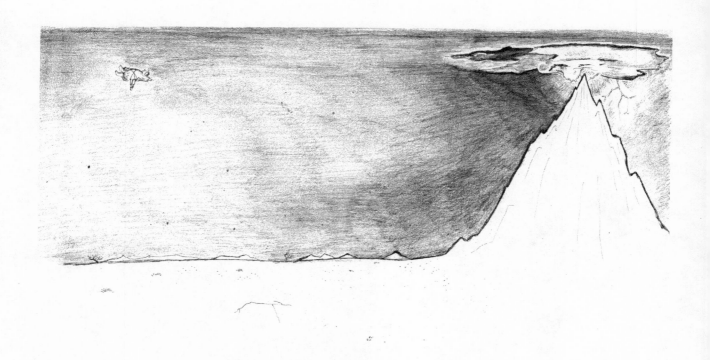

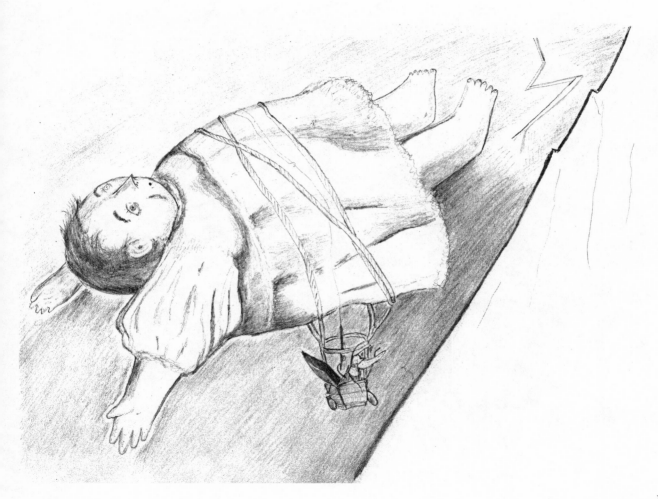

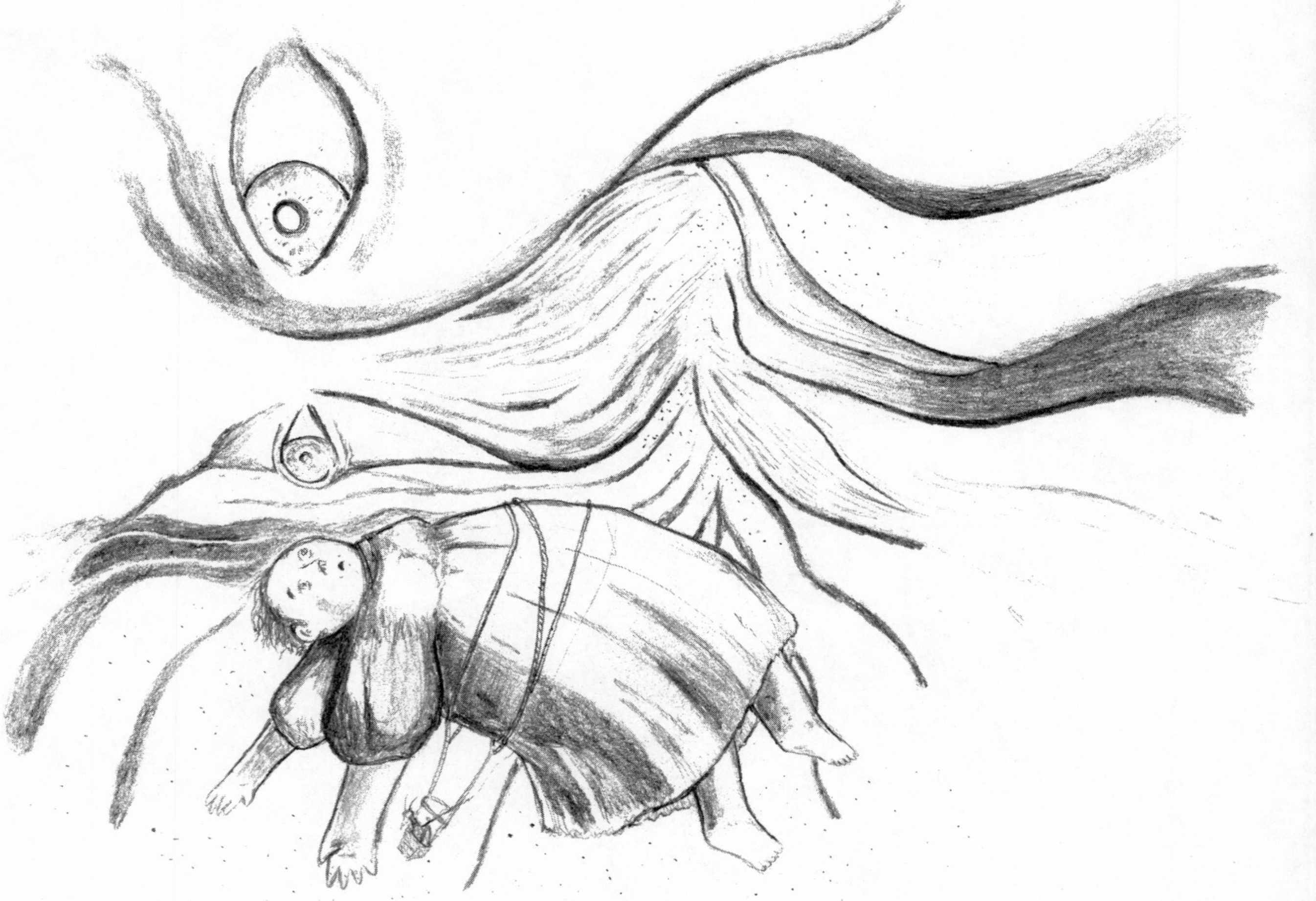

"HAVE YOU COME FOR RAIN?!" bellowed the Cloud.

But the girl could not speak.

"YOU DO NOT KNOW SUFFERING AS WE DO. WE HAVE ROAMED THE EARTH UNLOVED AND MEANINGLESS, HAUNTED BY THE LIVING."

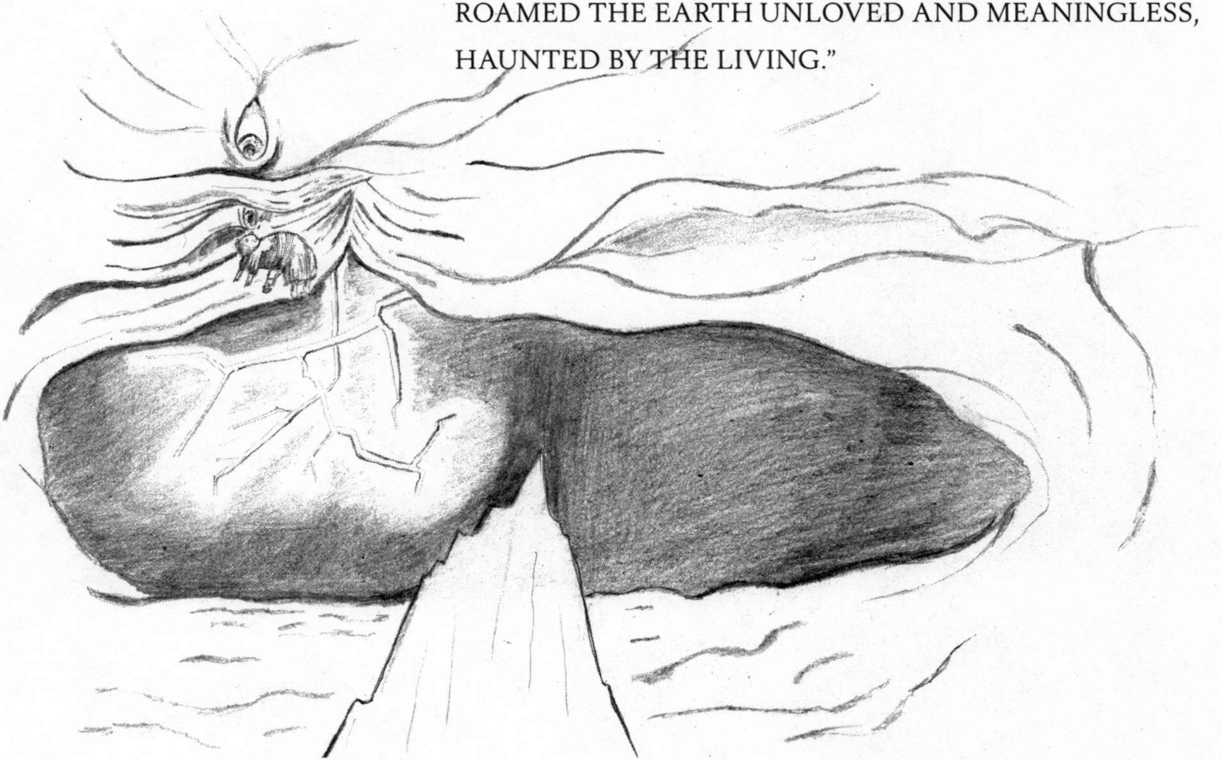

"TASTE OUR PAIN!!!" sang the Cloud as he filled the girl with his tears.

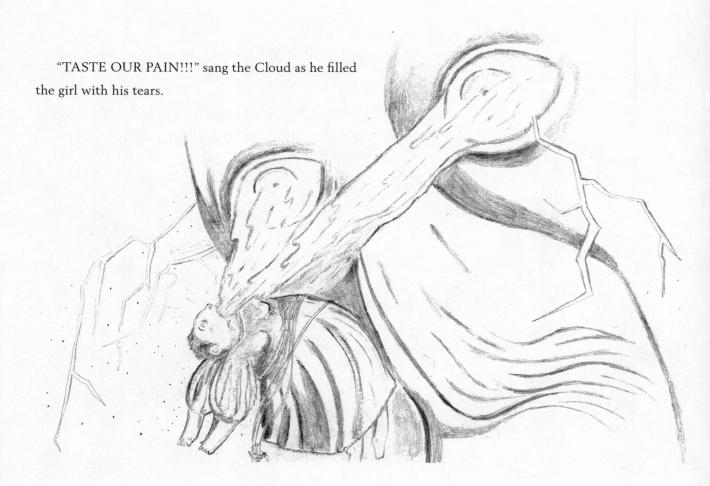

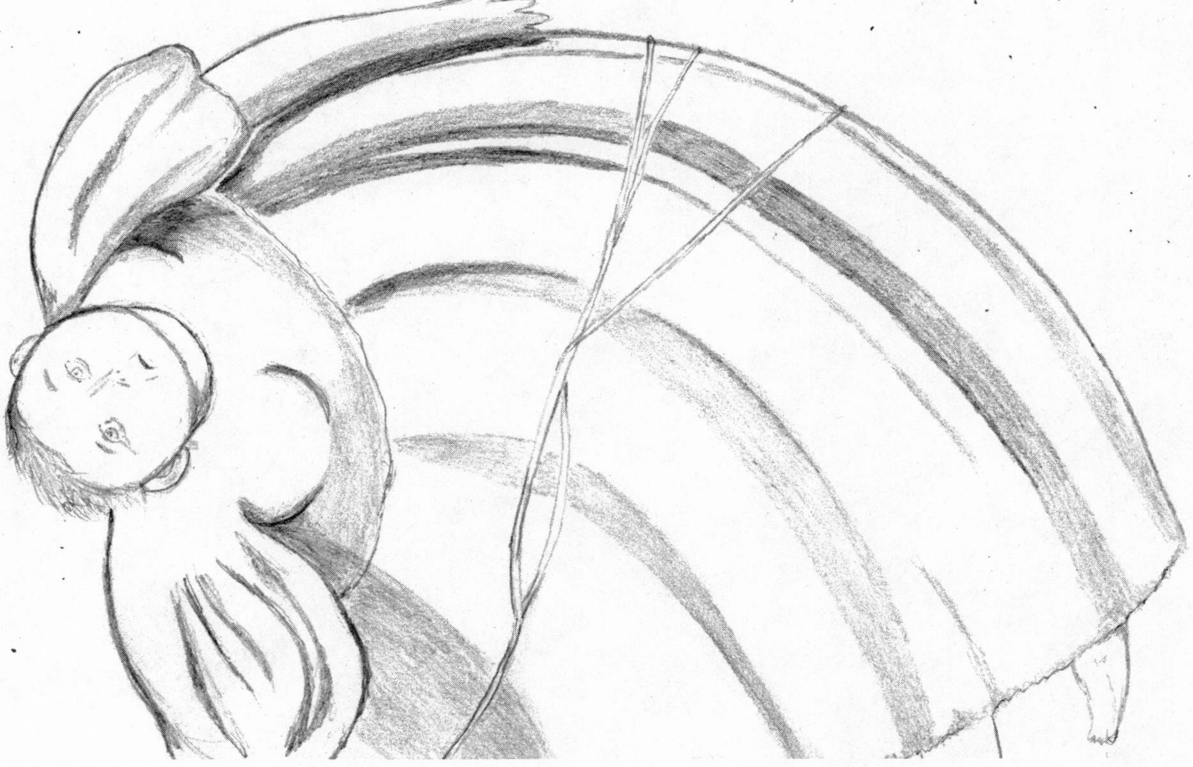

A rush of memories that the Cloud had held on to rushed through the girl as she drank down the Cloud's pain.

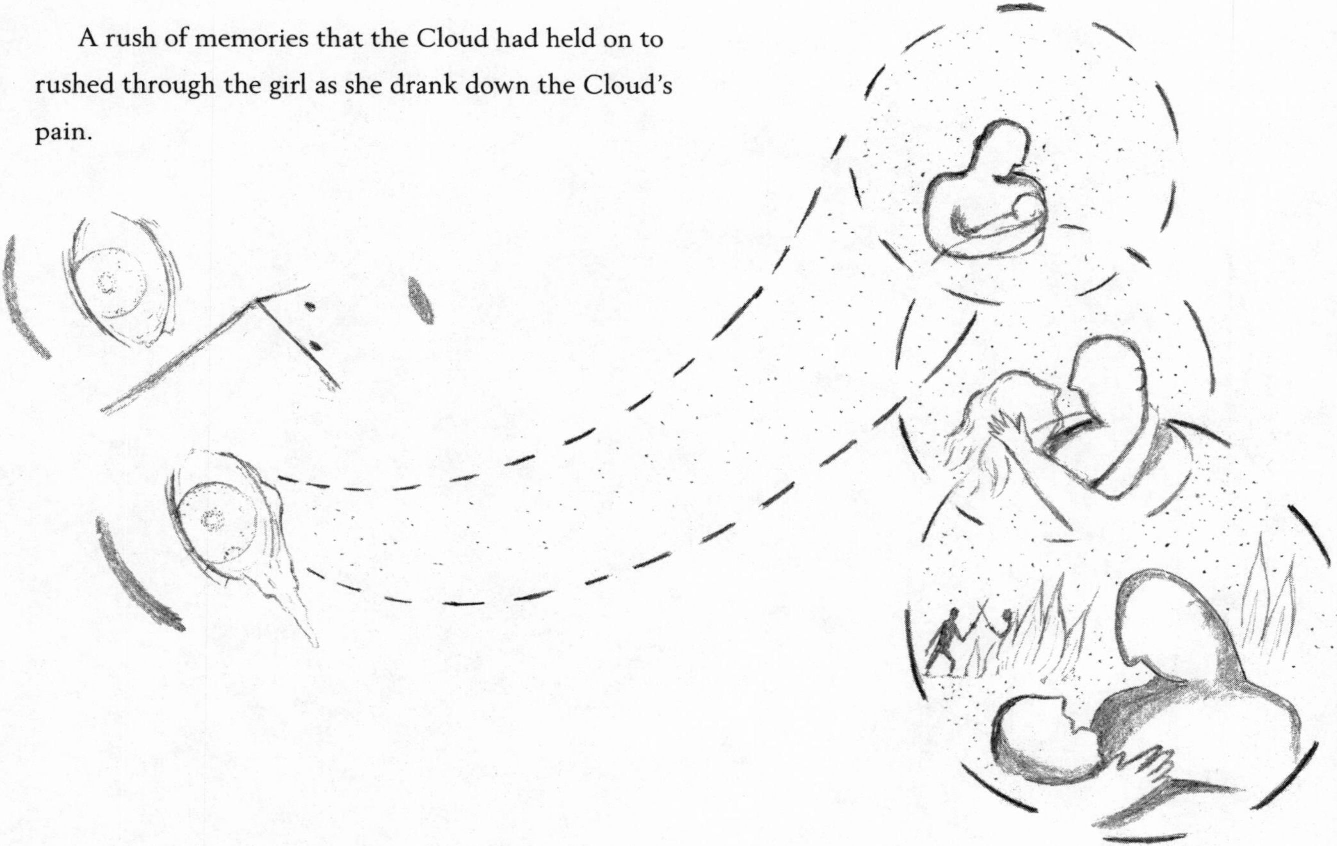

And then she spoke, "The people that loved you . . . the memories you shared . . . will always live with them."

She stared at the Cloud, "Will you tell that to my family as well?"

The knot in her throat loosened and untangled her sorrow, and she finally let out her rain.

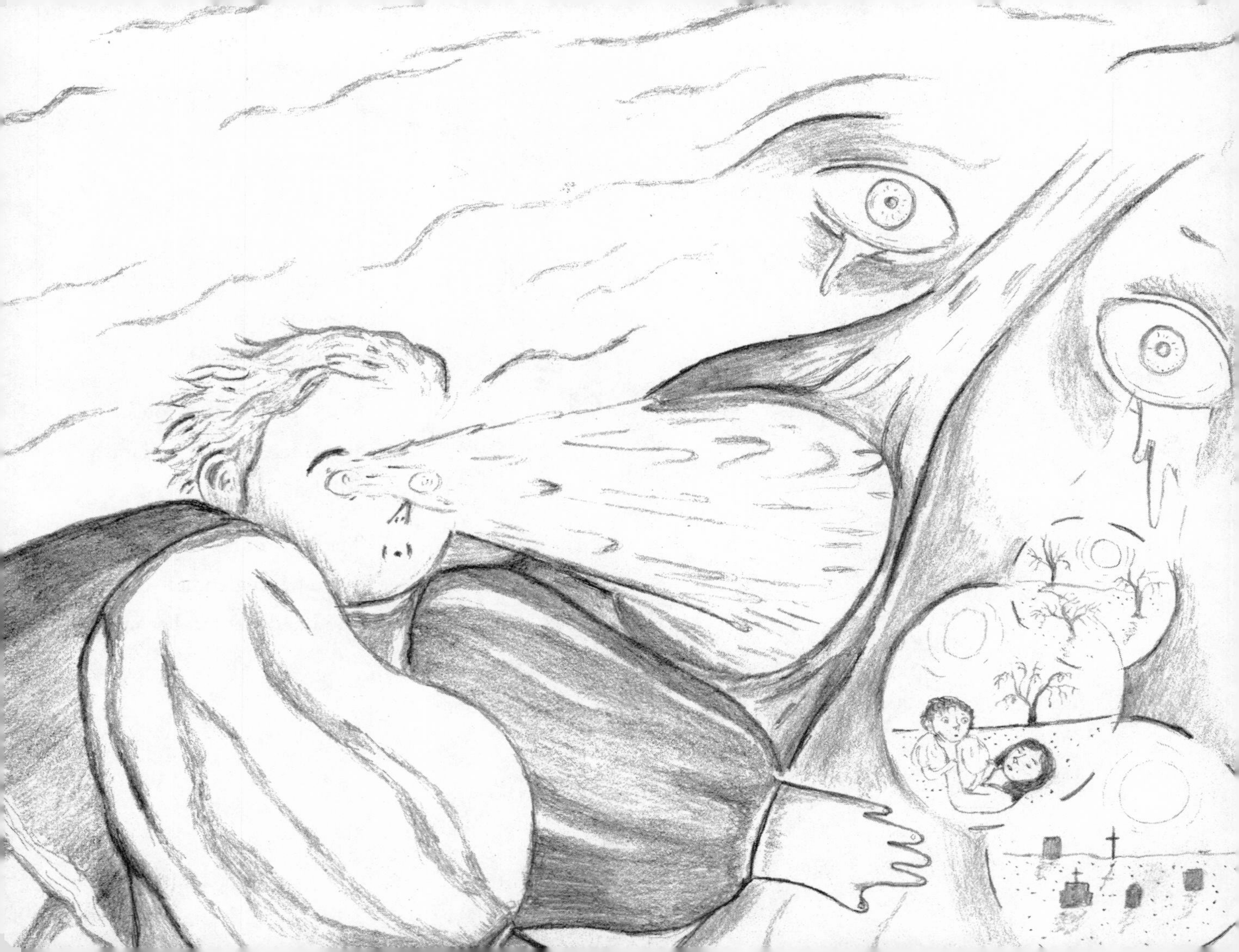

The other clouds gathered around.

" . . . We did not mean to carry on the cycle of pain. We did not mean for more death. We were foolish and hurt. We just wanted to feel important."

"You are, since the day you were born and forever more."

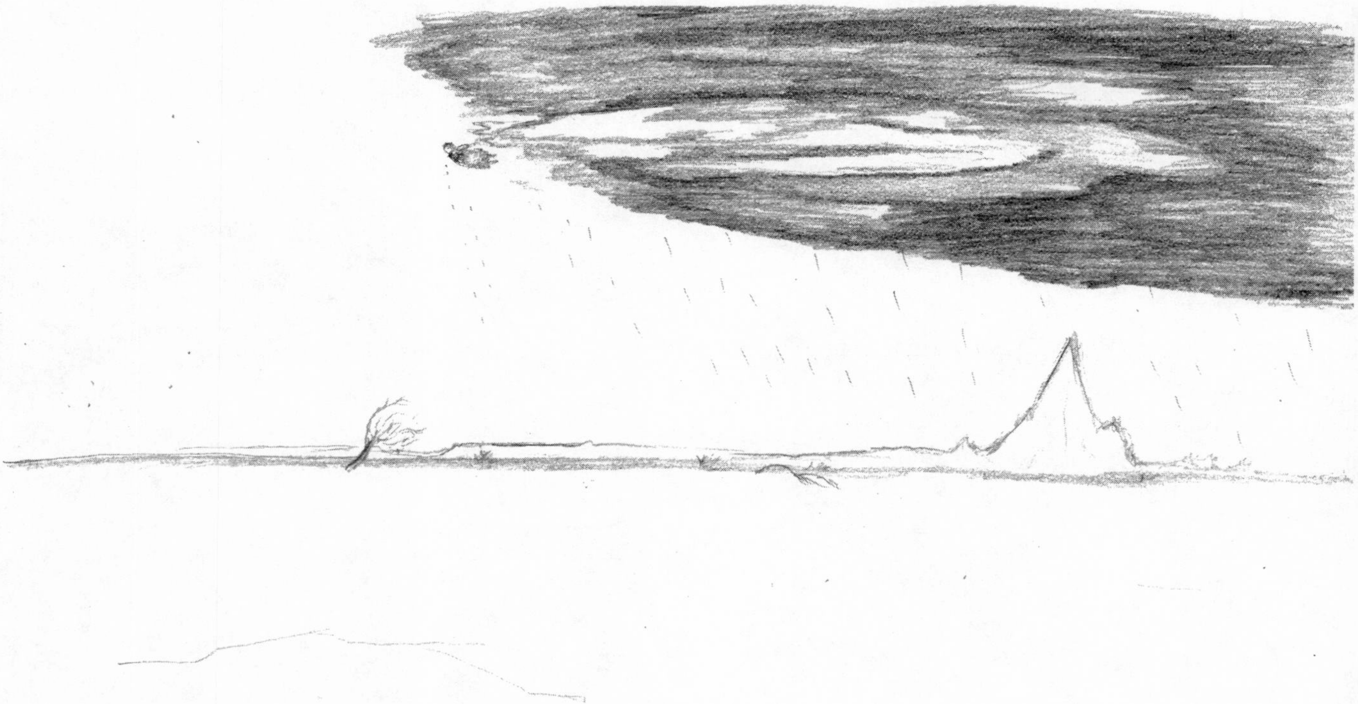

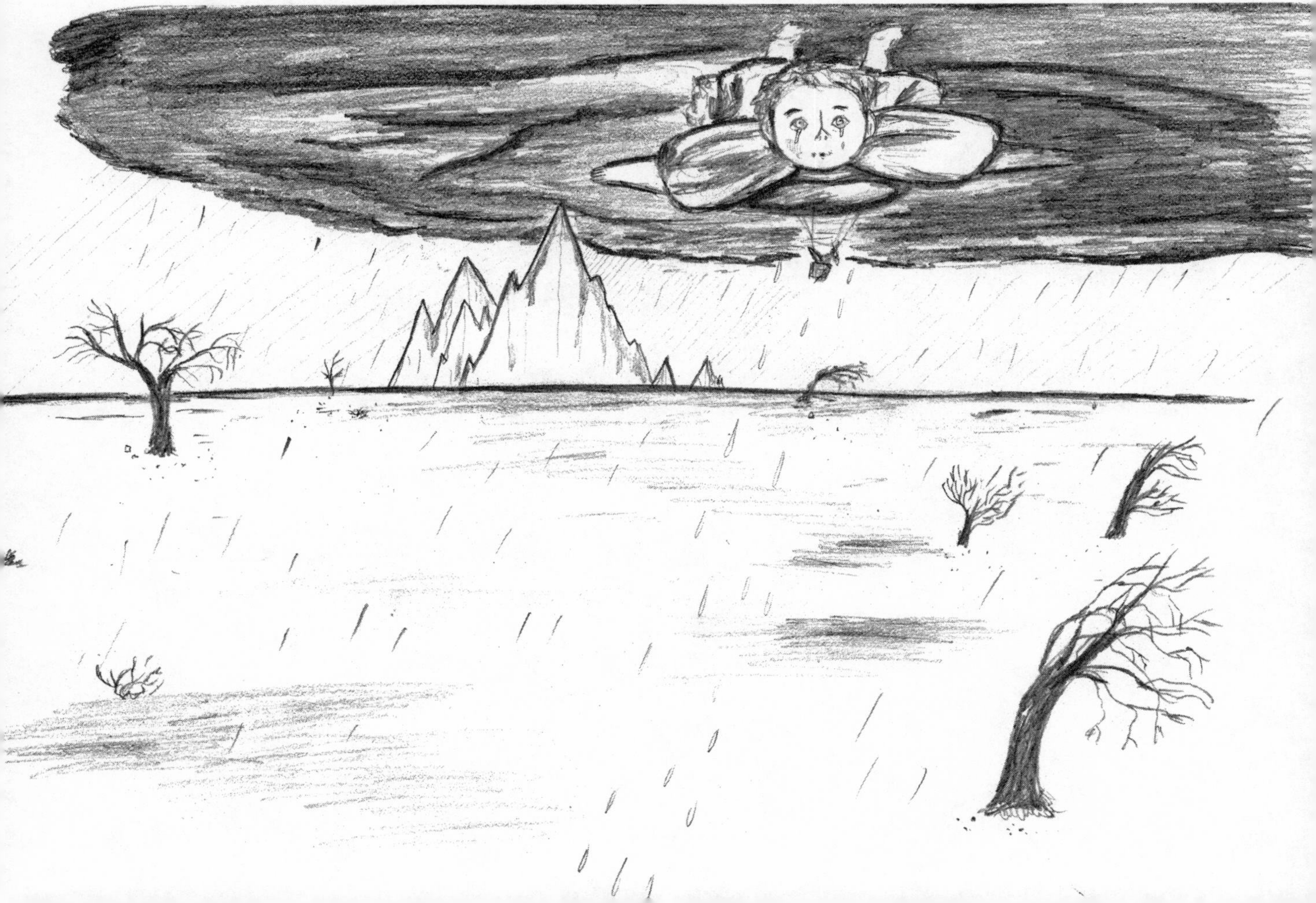

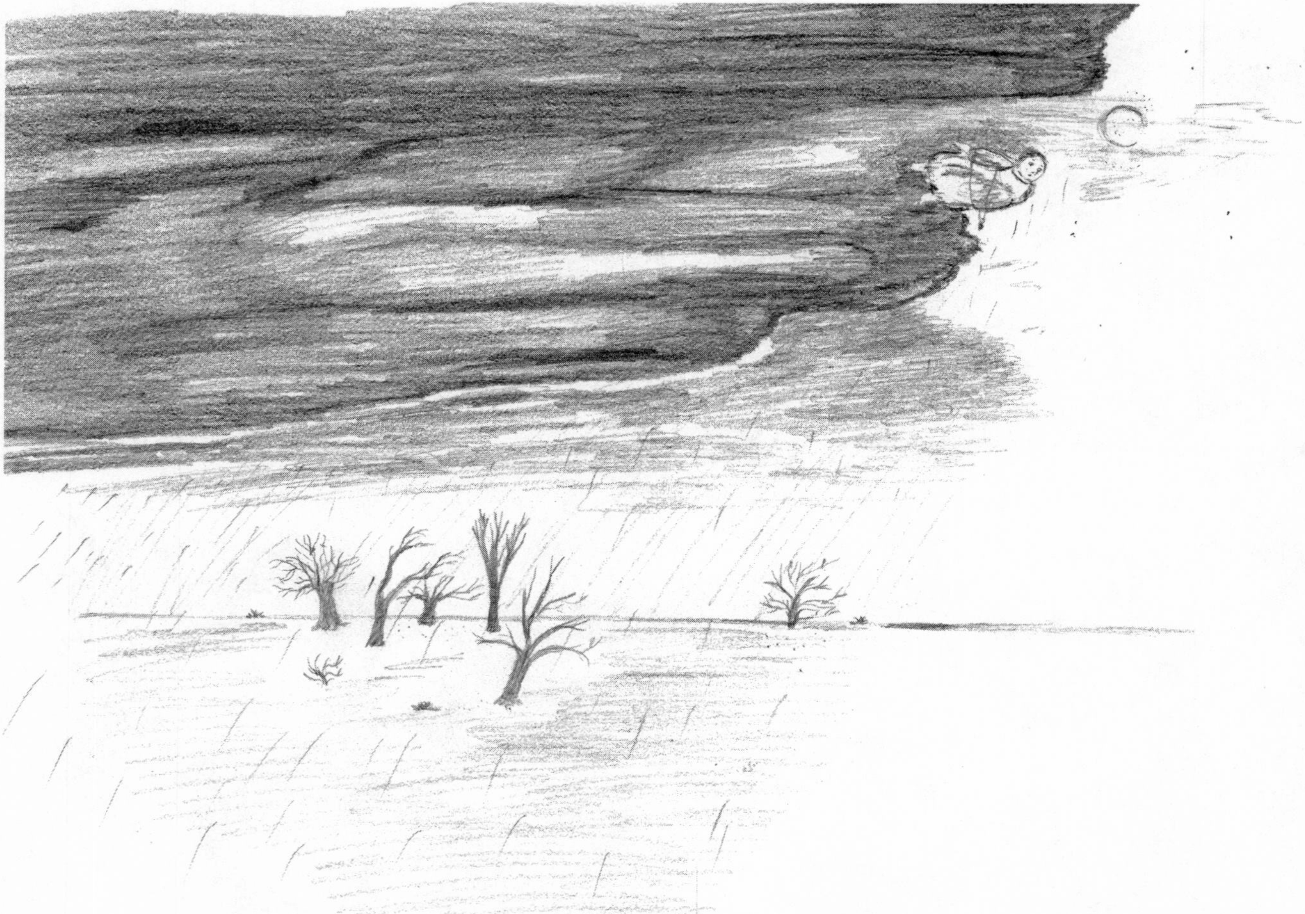

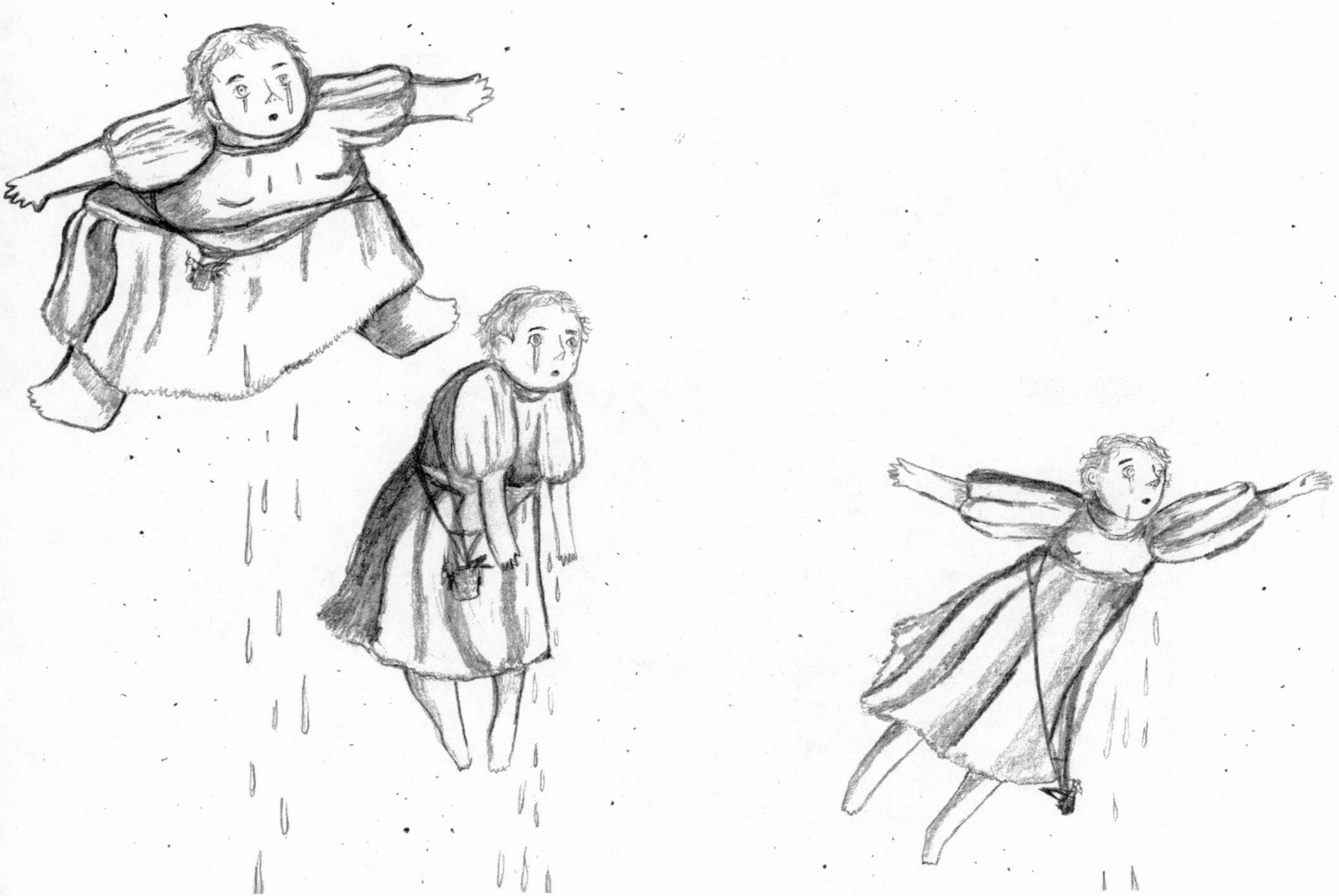

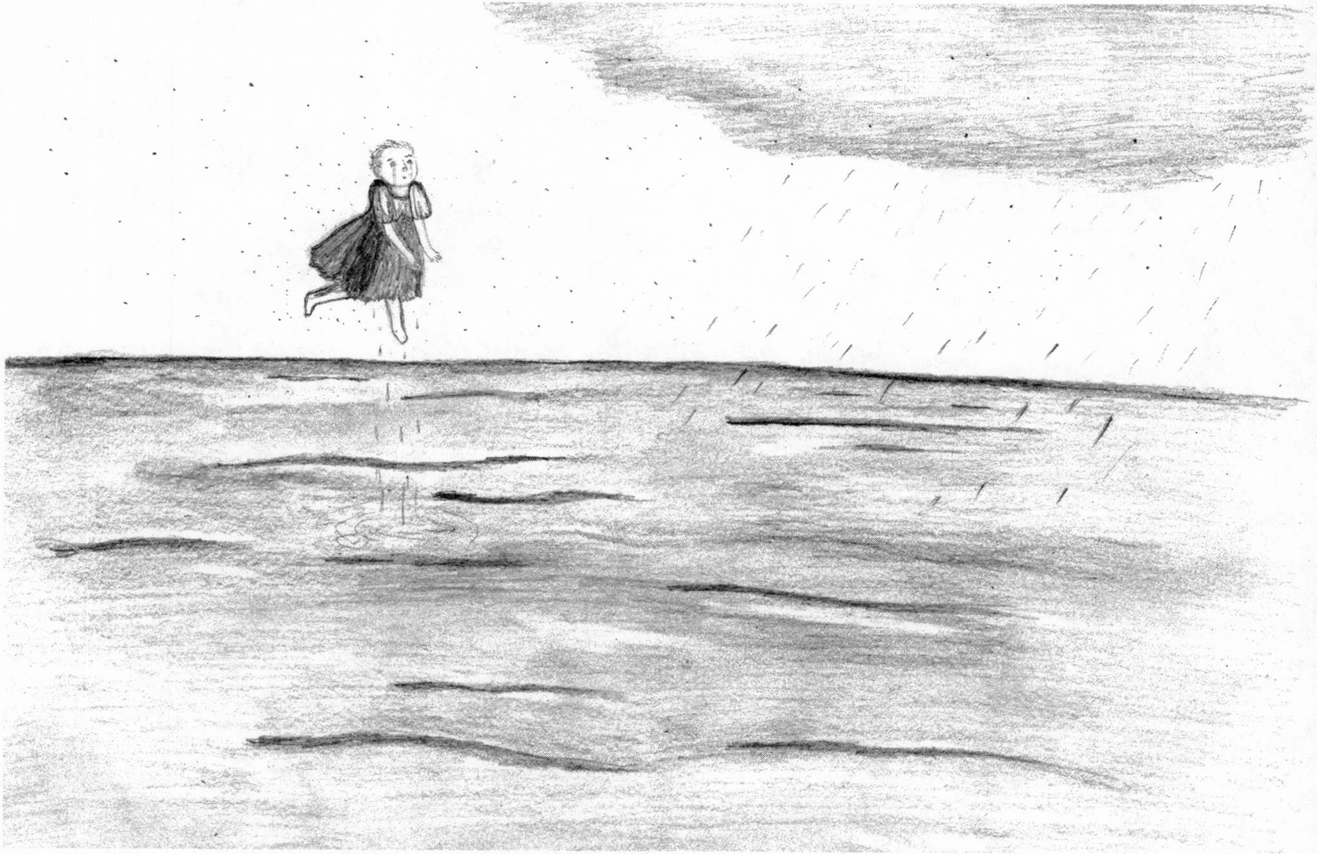

The clouds lost their darkness and dissipated into the world again.

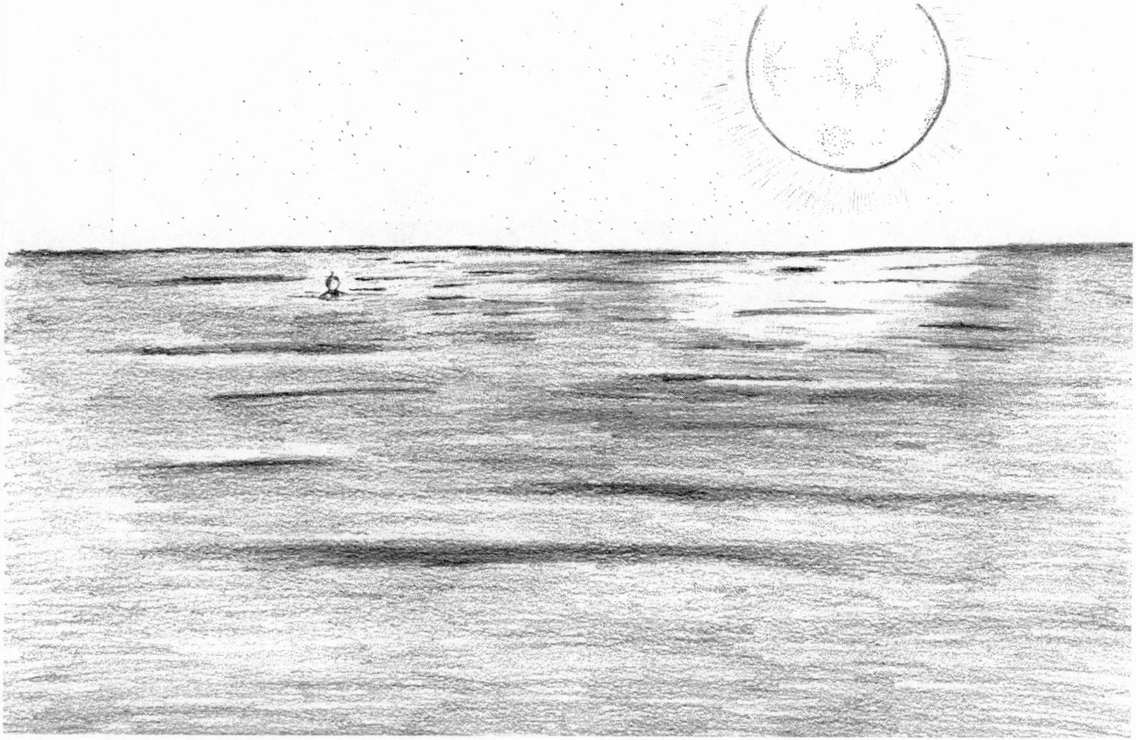

The end.

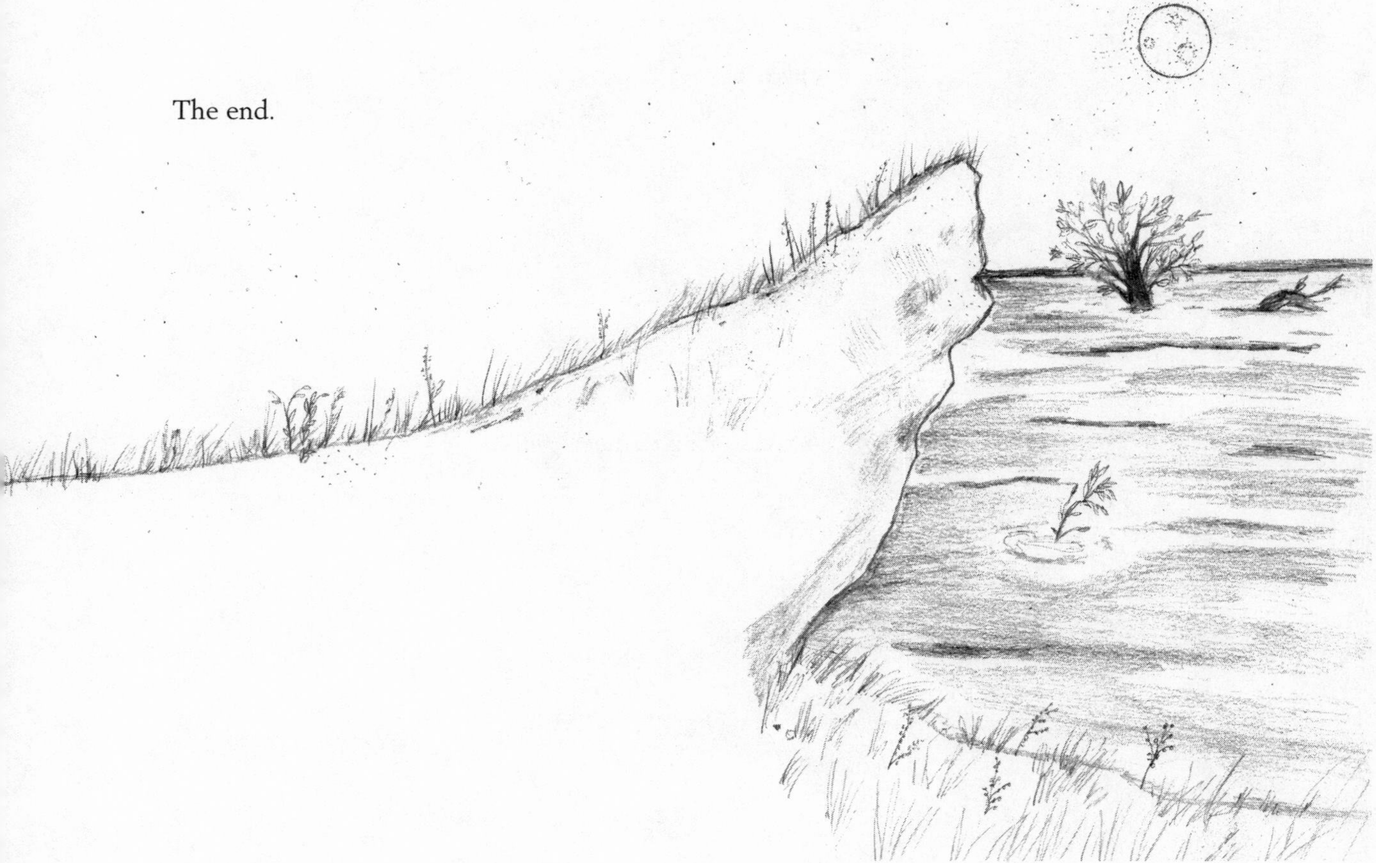

I've waited so long to meet you.

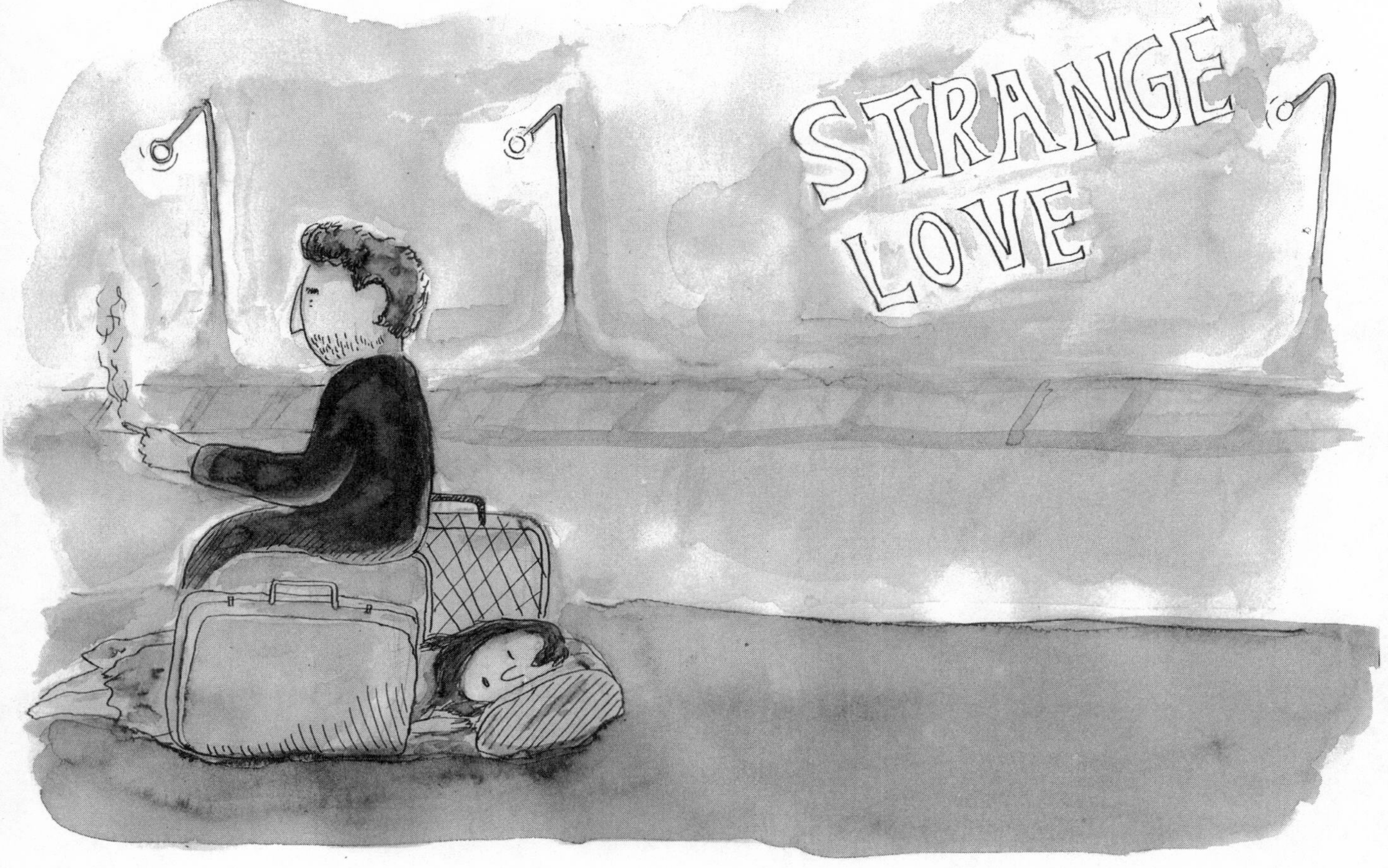
STRANGE
LOVE

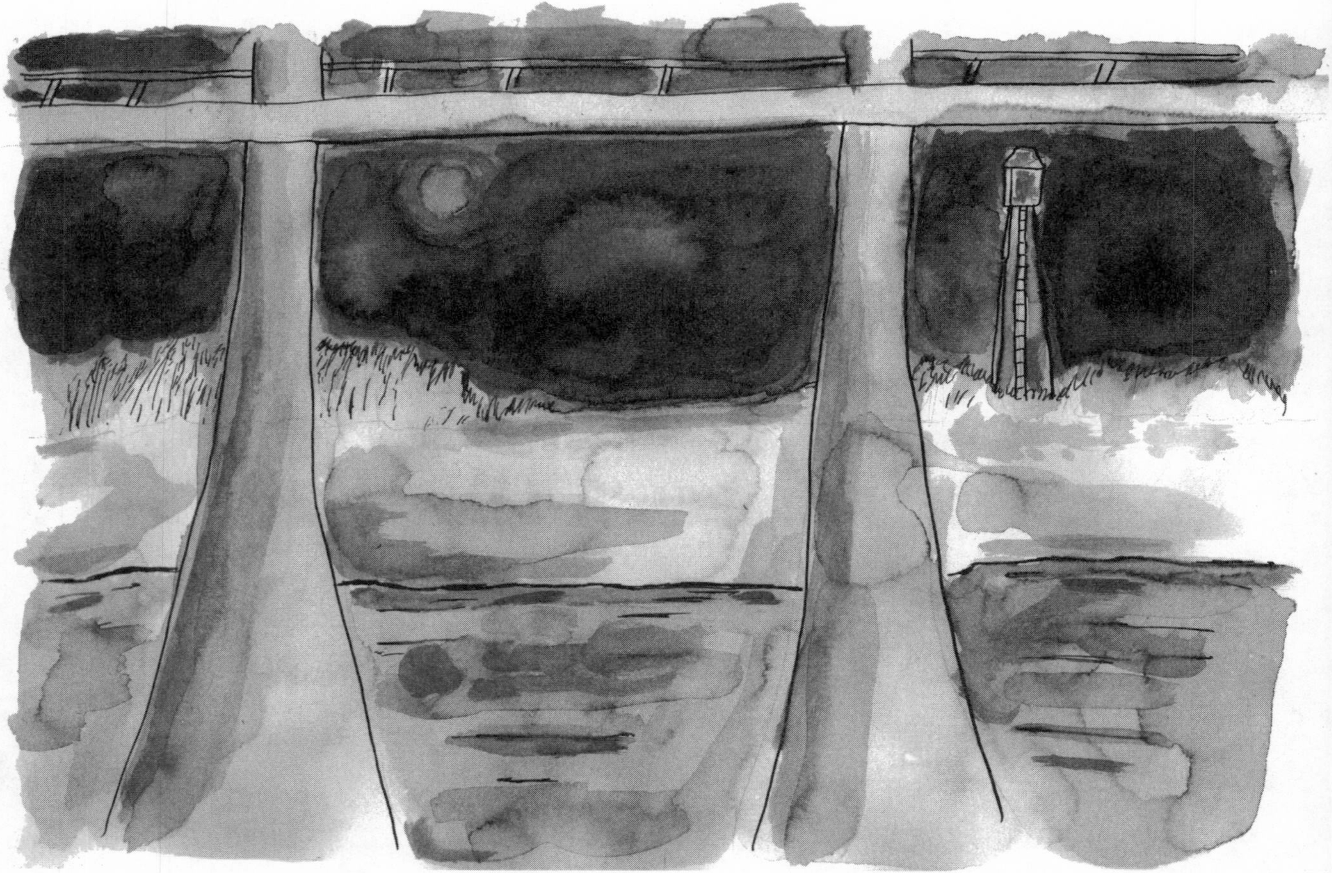

Forty-seven-year-old Leonard was drunk again.

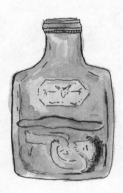

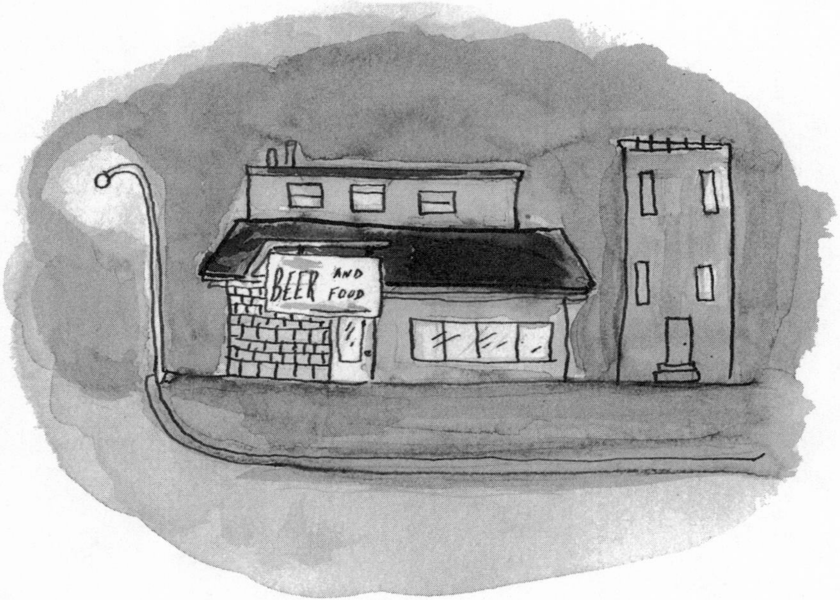
BEER AND FOOD

He hadn't slept for days, he'd forgotten how.

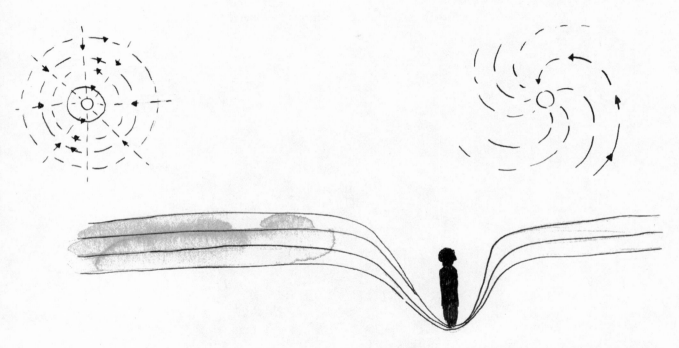

There are nights you run into pockets of gravity
heavier than others. Tonight, Leonard was in the
heaviest pocket of all.

He sat alone just like he had the night
before, practicing conversations he longed
to have.

Leonard entered the photo booth and pretended it was a time machine. He put three dollars in and hoped he could zoom himself into the future far from his sorrow.

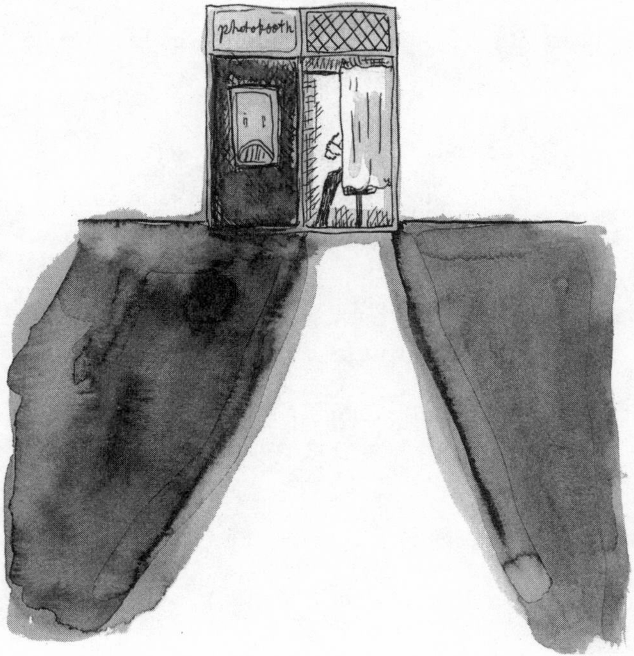
photobooth

Dizzy with whiskey, memories swam and circled him. Gravity seemed to have no mercy on Leonard's heart. It pressed so heavily on him, he felt as if he might burst into a billion pieces.

His thoughts raced, "If we are energy and energy cannot be created or destroyed—I WILL NOT BE DESTROYED."

A grenade of light flashed and shook Leonard, and at the exact moment his last photo was taken,

Leonard chose to live.

"I'm tired of self-destruction." The war inside him was over.
"It's time for a self-revolution!" And with that he decided to
celebrate with another drink.

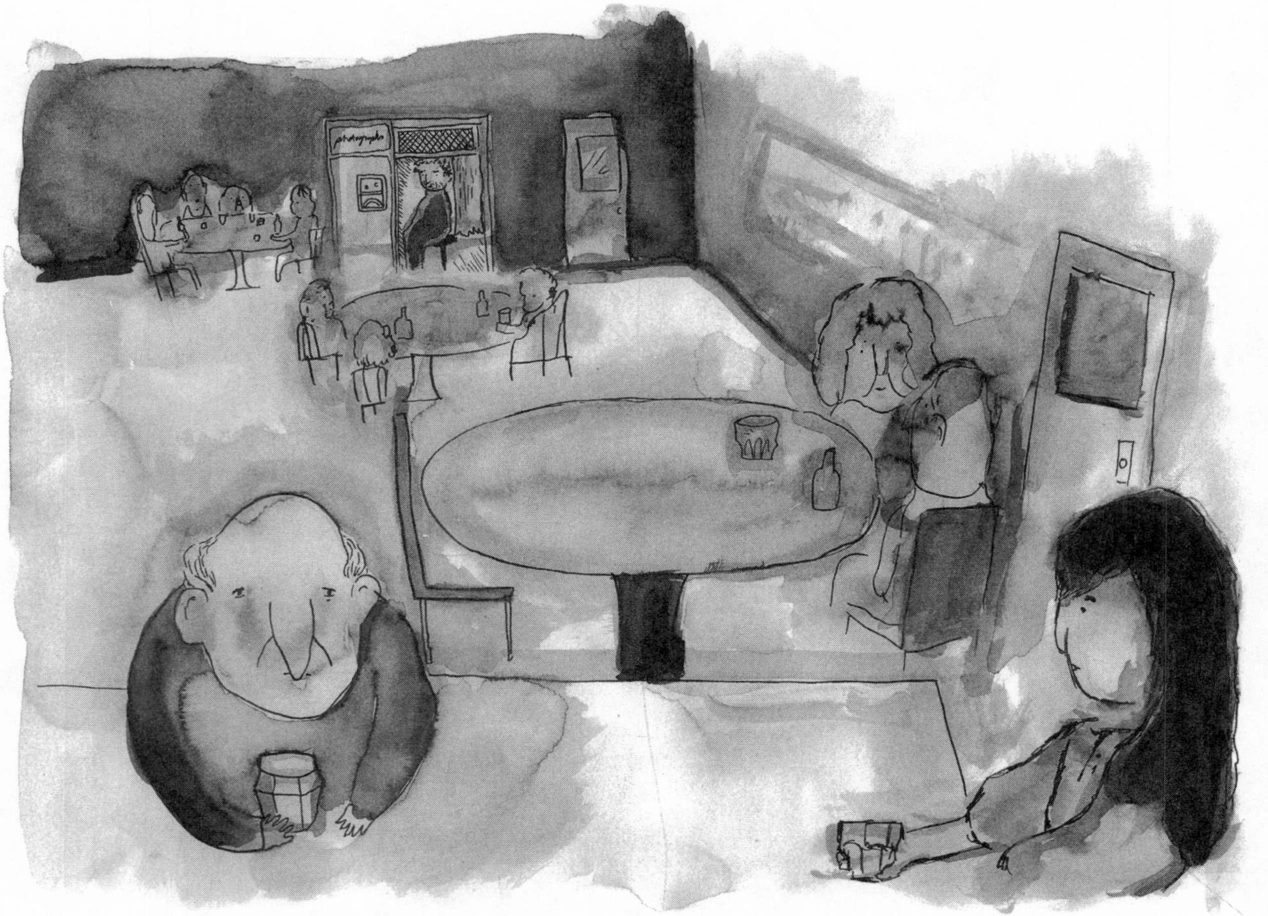
photographs

Leonard locked eyes with a stranger.

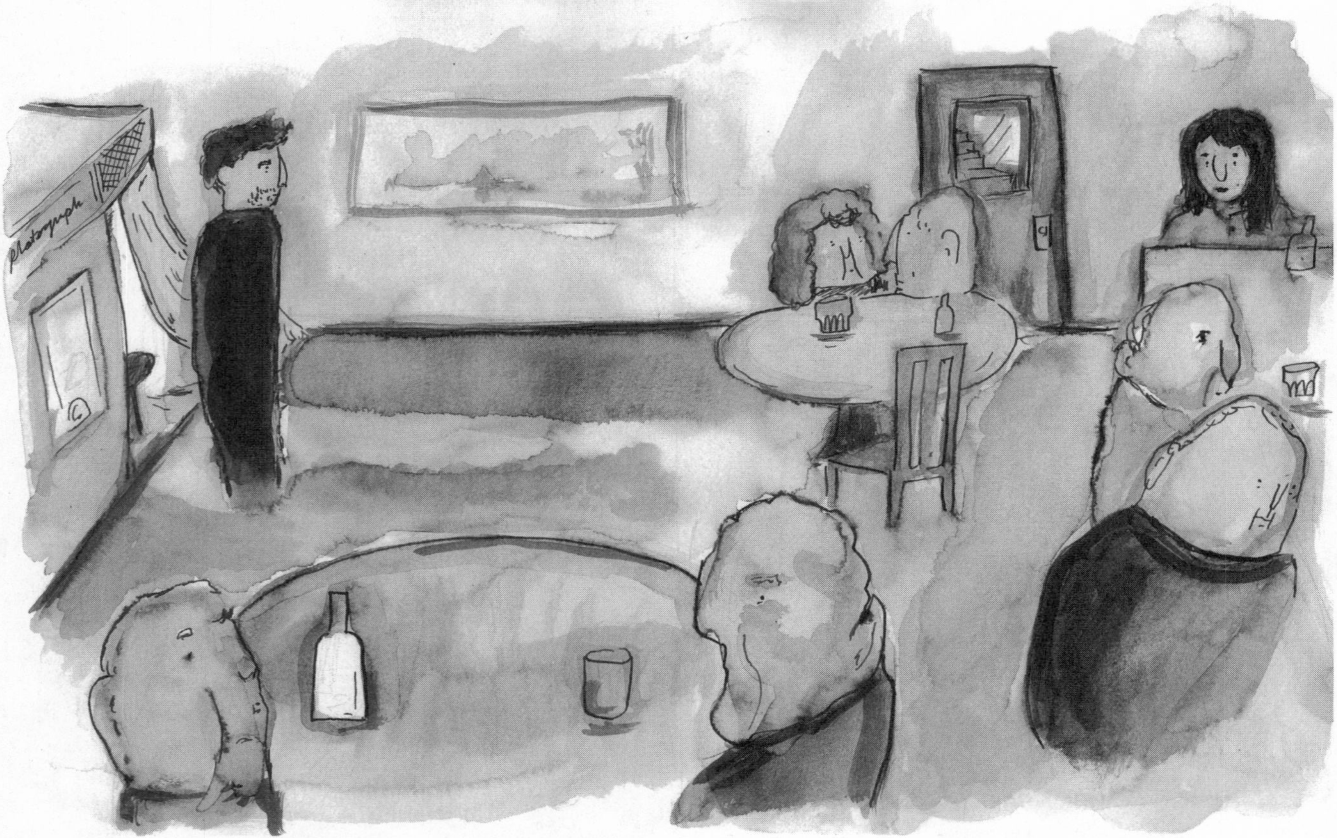
Photograph

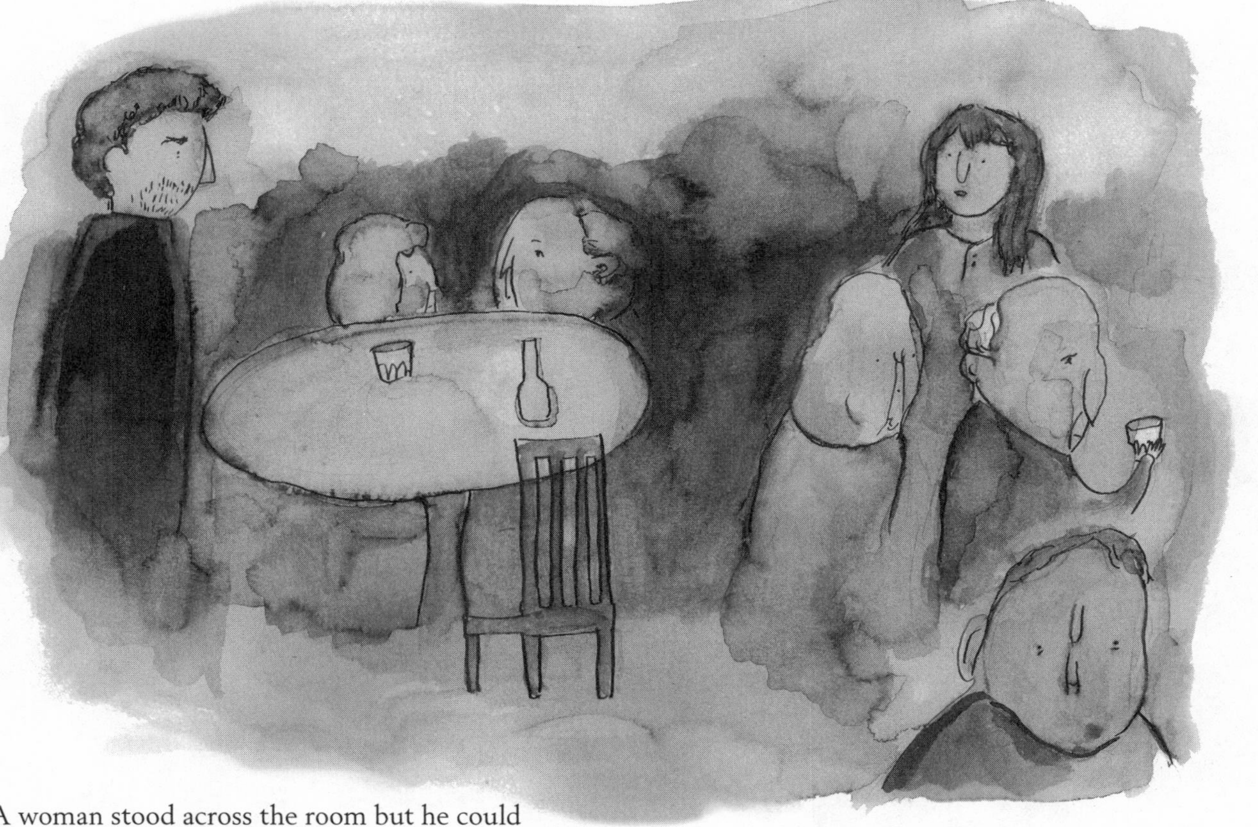

A woman stood across the room but he could feel space and distance becoming less relevant.

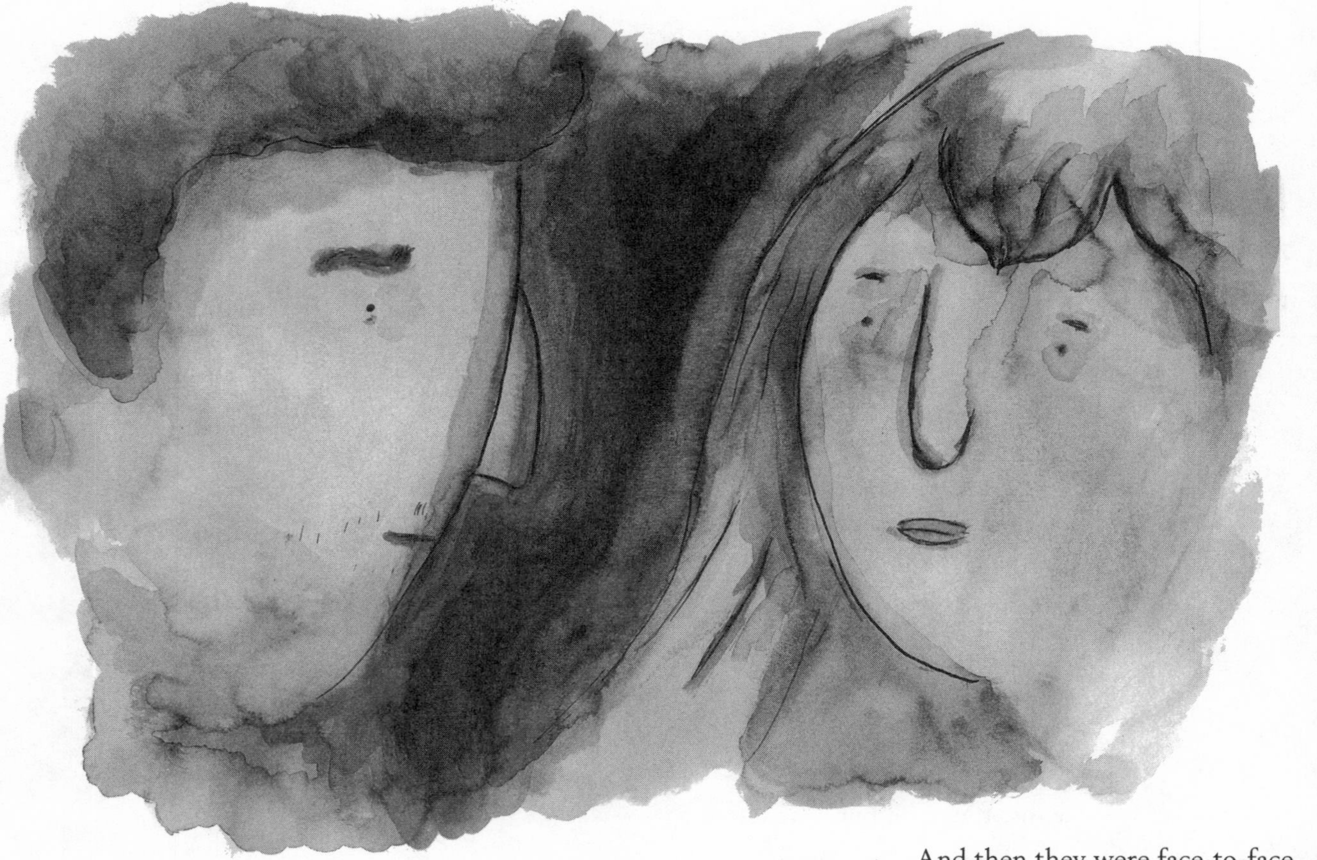

And then they were face-to-face.

"I can't tell if you're staring at me because you wanna ask me to dance, or if you're trying to make my head explode."

"Maybe a little of both. I'm Leonard."

"Marie."

"I like how your soul bends your face."

Her face became stone, "I've got a lot of baggage."

Leonard smiles, "Don't worry, I've got a pickup truck."

"I don't know." She stood up and indeed had a lot of baggage.

"You weren't kidding."

She started to walk away.

"Now wait a minute, I've got baggage too. And it's not every day I meet someone so honest. I'd like a chance to get to know you before you just walk out of my life forever."

Marie stopped. She turned around and stared at Leonard, "Okay."

"You'll go on a walk with me?"

She nodded, "Okay."

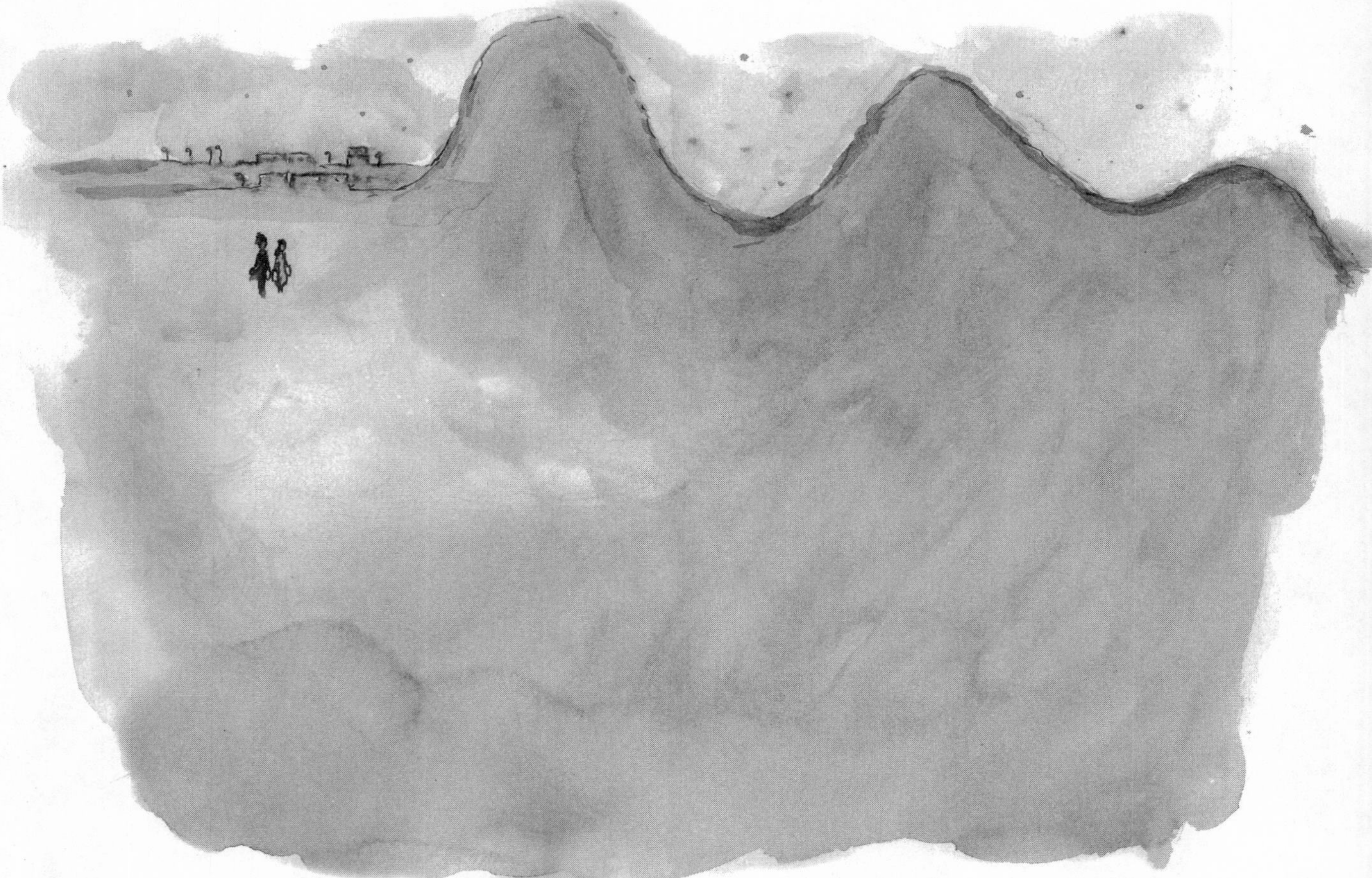

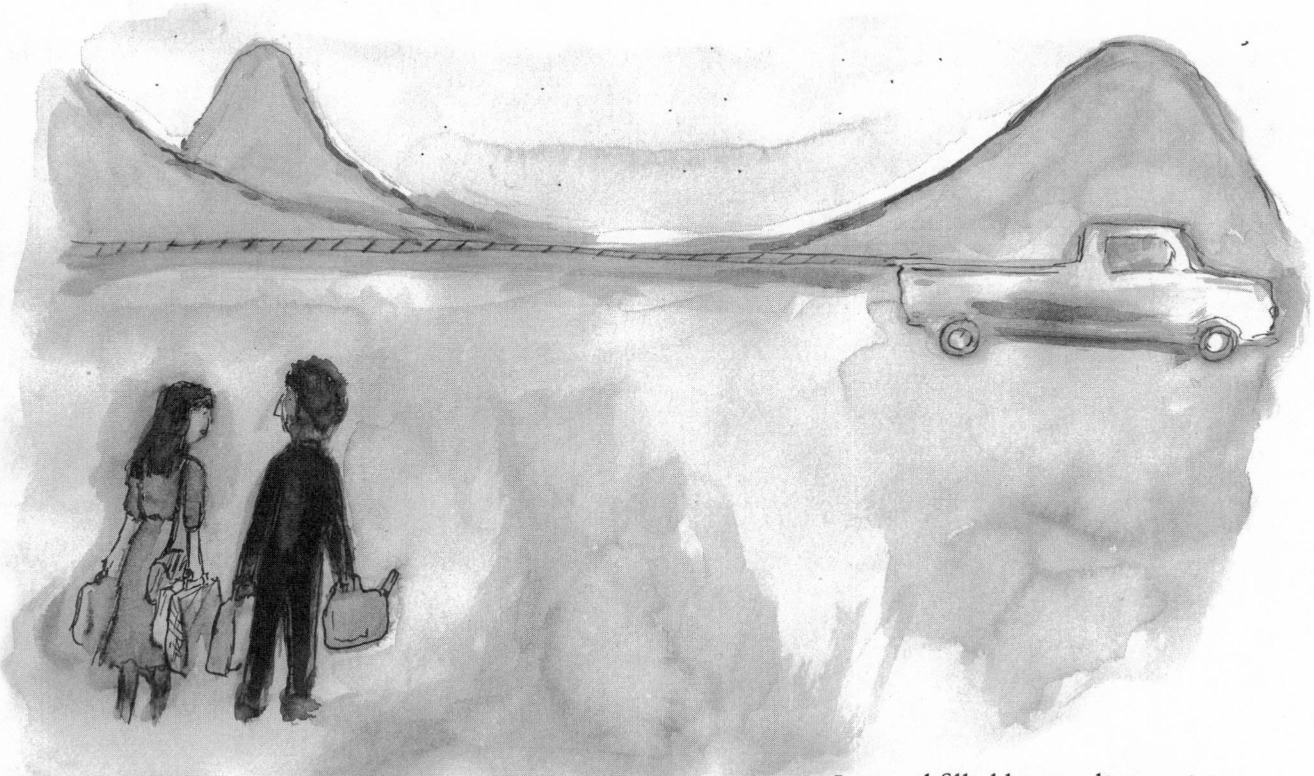

Leonard filled his gasoline canister for his truck.

Marie wobbled, trying to keep her balance on the train tracks. "I hope you don't think this is going to lead to anything. I'm too old for love."

"I hope you're not planning on bringing your baggage with us. If you're as old as you claim, you don't wanna throw your back out on our first date. We may not have a second." He took her baggage and placed it in the back of his truck.

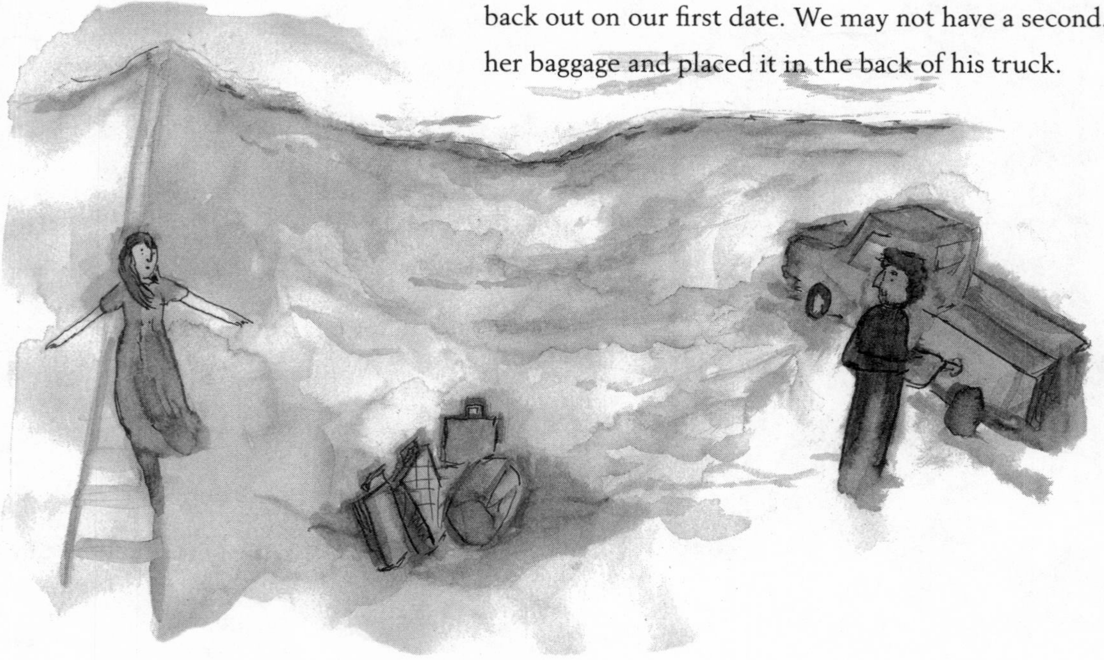

Marie took a deep breath, "I don't know how to small talk."

"I don't know how to talk."

They stared at each other.

"I had a wife once. One day I looked at her and could tell she didn't love me anymore. I stopped looking into her eyes after that."

"I ignored it for as long as I could. Like a child who accidentally broke his mom's favorite vase, I turned my shoulder because I didn't want it to be true."

"I tried to make her love me again—you can't make someone love you. It's magic. We had grown apart, she changed and I stayed exactly the same. Eventually she'd had enough so she held her heart against my head like a gun and pleaded, 'Let me go.' . . . So I did."

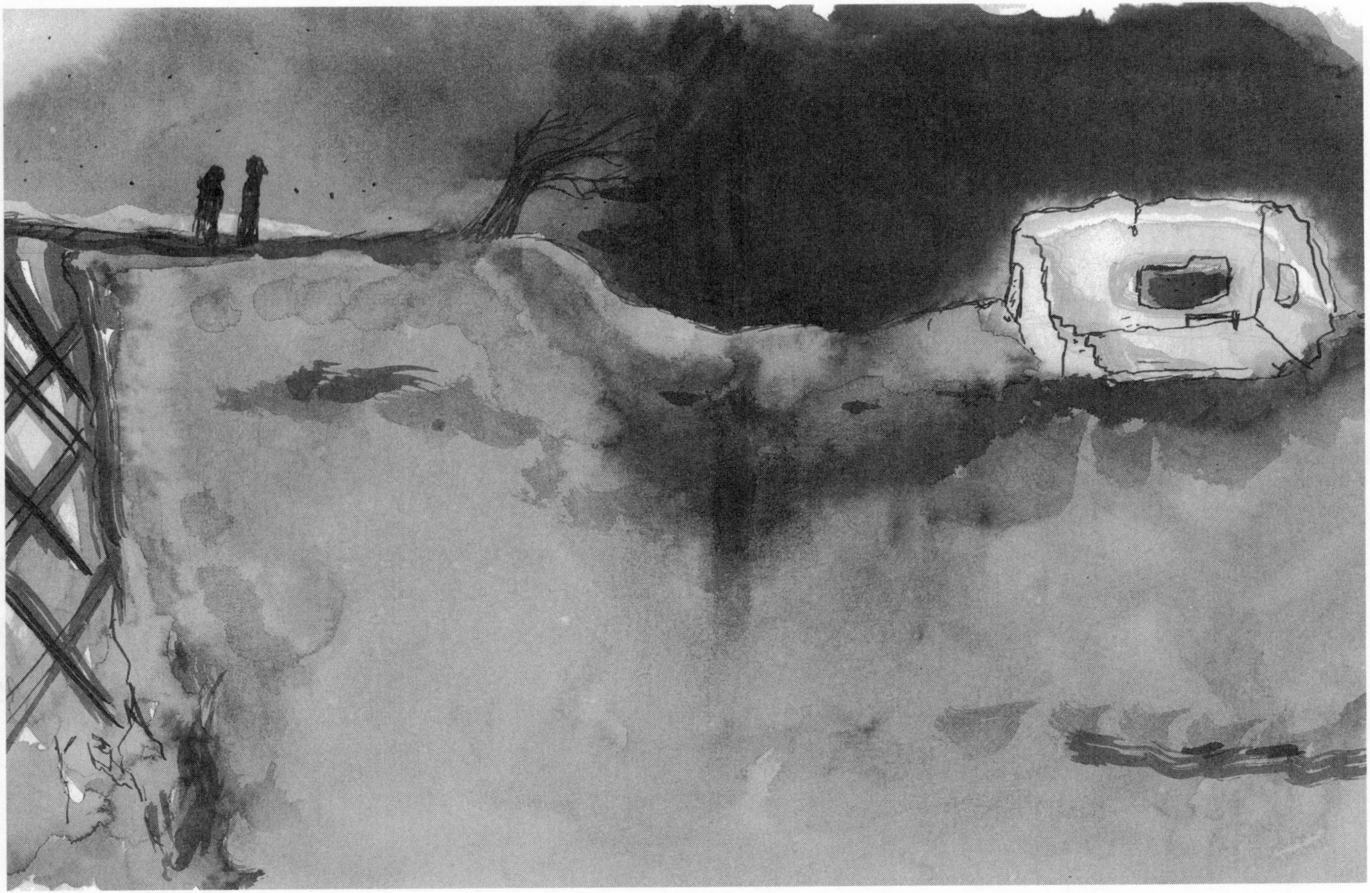

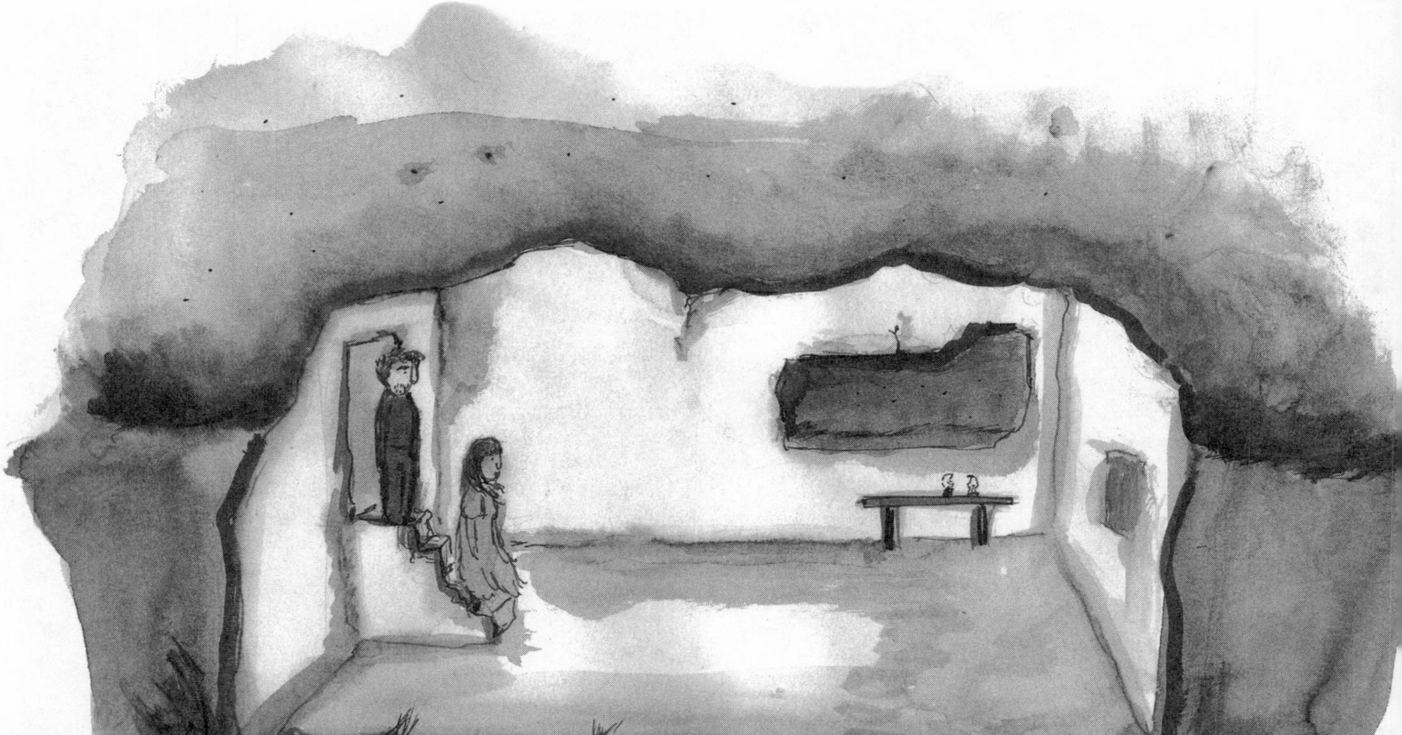

"The guy I was in love with—we had a long-distance kinda thing. You know that part in *Peter Pan* when Peter flies through the window and hasn't seen Wendy in a long time? Wendy's back is turned toward Peter and he's so excited to surprise her but when he grabs her shoulder Peter is so horrified to find out that Wendy is old that he faints three times and throws up. It sucks for Wendy because she has to clean up after him. The poor dame is so old that her back gives up and she dies . . . I hope I didn't ruin the story for you."

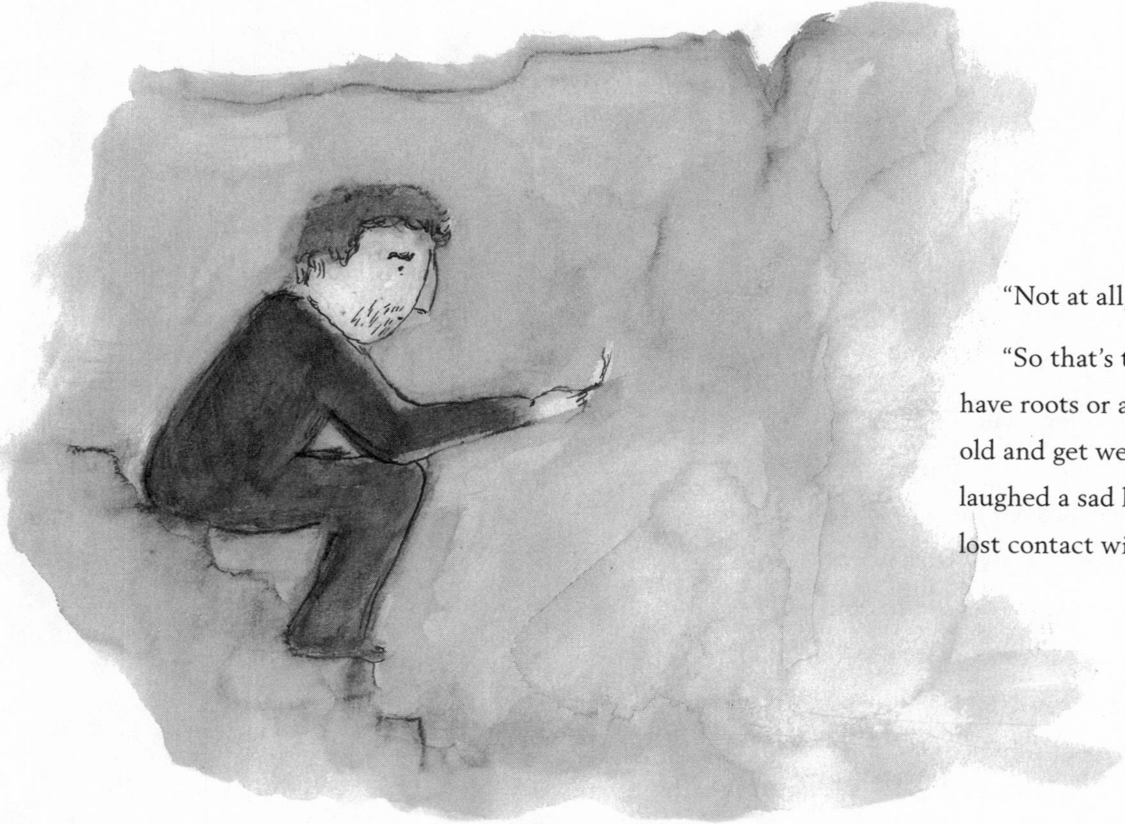

“Not at all,” Leonard smiled.

“So that’s the gist. He didn’t have roots or any desire to grow old and get weird with me.” She laughed a sad laugh and her eyes lost contact with Leonard’s.

"You know what I'd like to do more than anything right now?"

"What?"

"I'd like to take the rest of that gasoline and light your baggage in flames so I could watch all the pain in your eyes roll out and your face light up. And when there's nothing but dust, I'd look back in your eyes and see that your heart was free, and that you were really looking back at me."

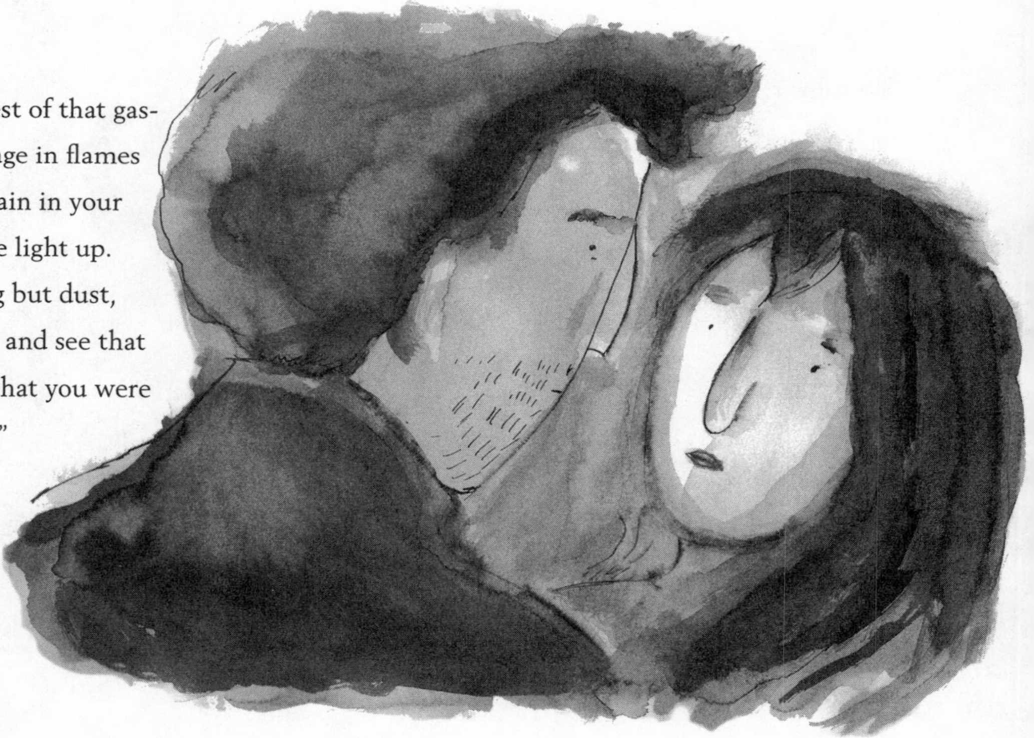

Marie pulled back, afraid of a kiss, "What do you think happened to those snow globes?"

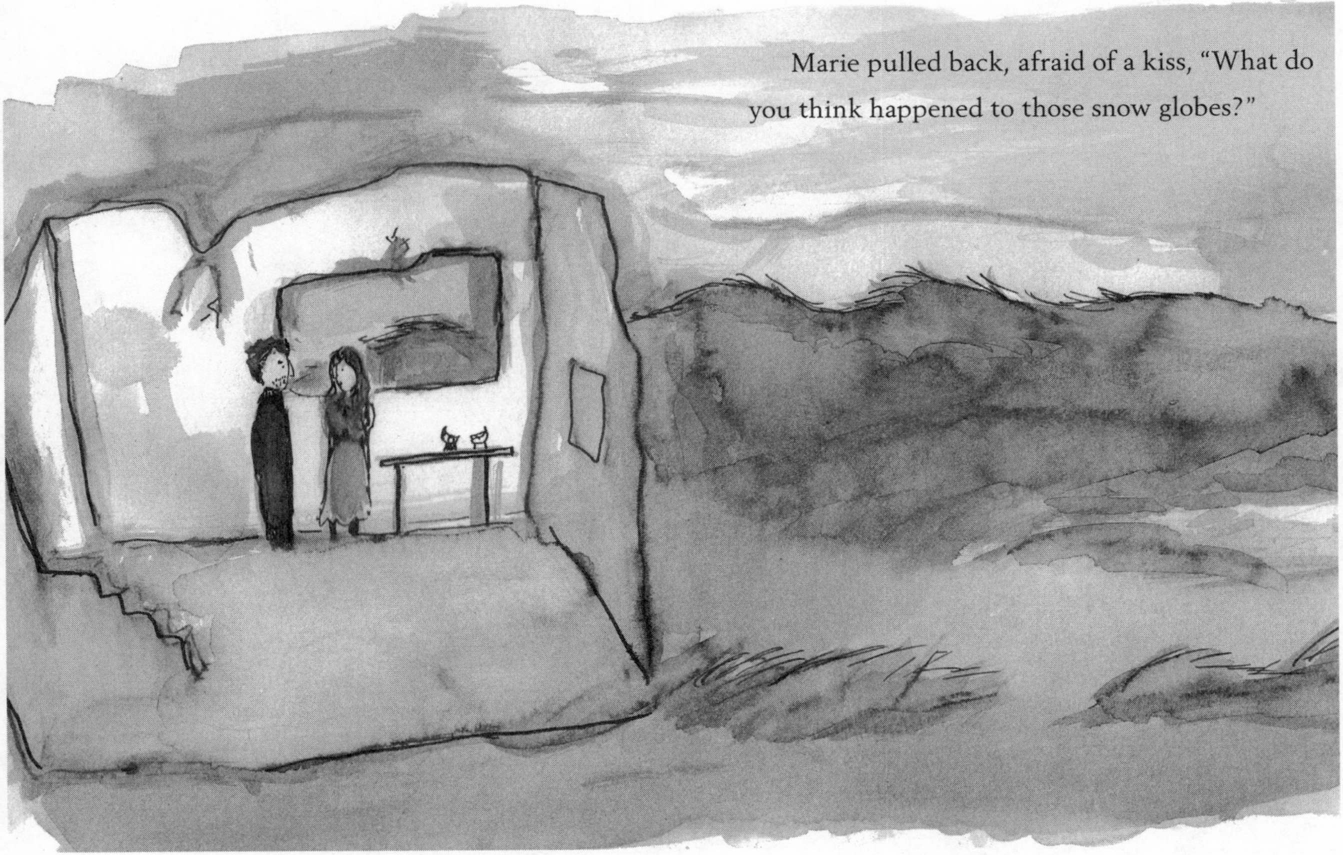

Leonard looked closer, “I think they fought for love and won.”

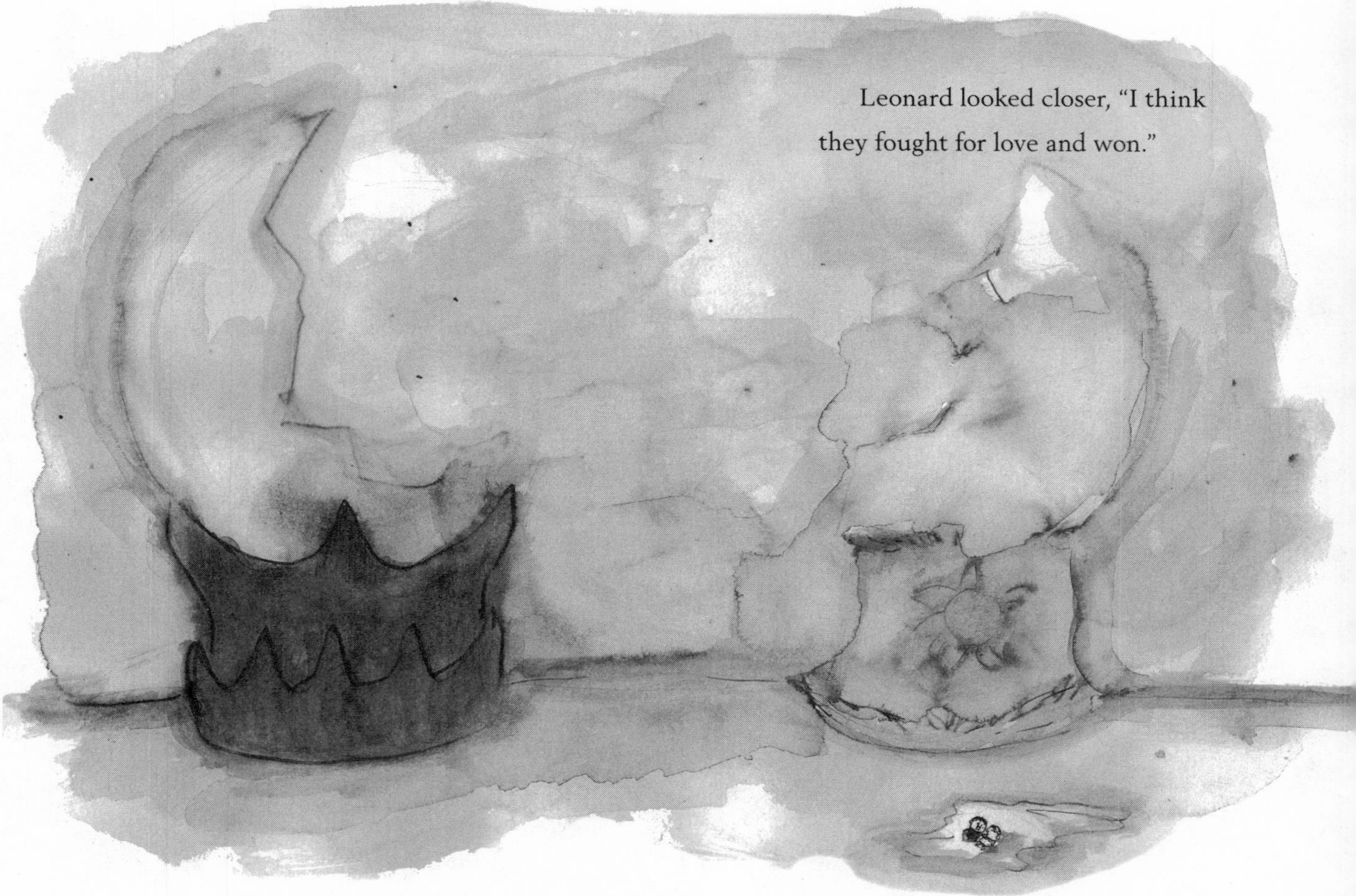

"Maybe we should head back," said Marie.

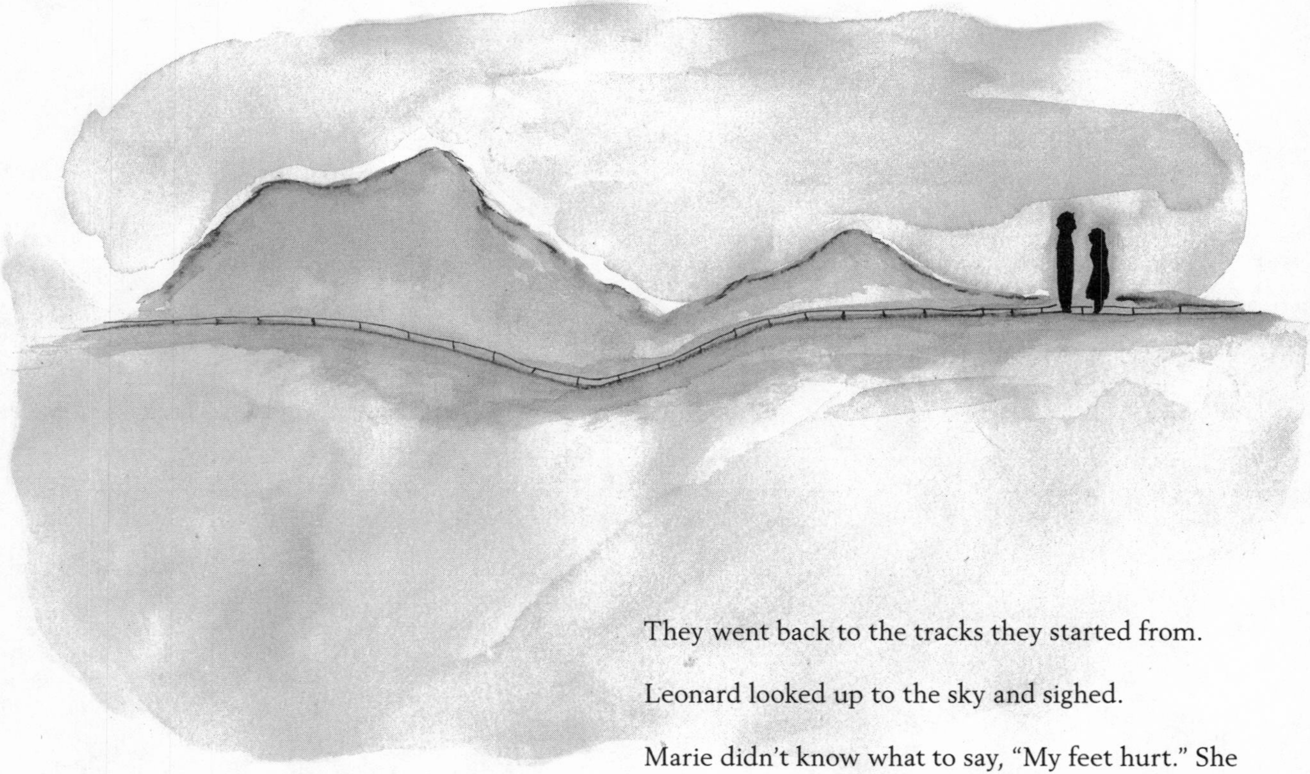

They went back to the tracks they started from.

Leonard looked up to the sky and sighed.

Marie didn't know what to say, "My feet hurt." She walked to the truck, climbed onto it, and lay on her back.

Leonard joined her.

Marie closed her eyes, "Whenever a baby or dog stares at me, I get nervous they can see something secret and deep inside me."

"You must get especially nervous when baby dogs are around."

Marie laughed.

"What do you think they can see?"

"Dunno. Maybe my soul? When they bark or cry, I feel like they can see something evil in me. I feel like your eyes might have the same powers."

She looked afraid.

"I'm pregnant." Wind blew around Marie.

"Don't worry . . . I've got a pickup truck."

Her face was heavy but she smiled a heavy smile, "I was right about those eyes of yours . . ."

She looked at him deeply as if searching
for something, "I don't want to get hurt."

"I don't want to either."

"Oh, Leonard, I think we met too late."

"What do you mean?"

"I wish we had met when we were young and I wasn't
so broken. I wish we were in love and could overcome
anything." Marie started to cry.

"Who says we're not in love?"

"Please don't do this. Don't play games with
me."

"Marie, stay with me." He held her face in
the palm of his hand.

“Don’t go getting so lost in your own head that I can’t reach you. I’ve worked so hard in my life to destroy things, things that were important to me. Open your eyes, look at me . . .” She did. “I want to fall madly in love with you, and I swear to God if you gave us a chance, our love would be so strong it could never be destroyed.”

She held him tight, “Thank you for finding me, Leonard.”

“Everything’s going to be okay, I’ve got you.”

She held him even tighter.

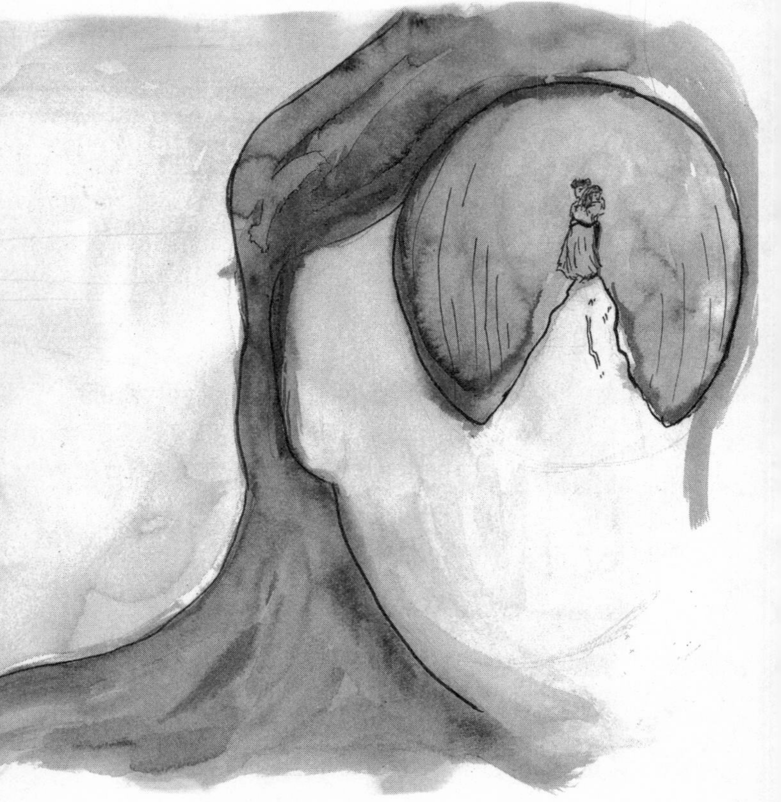

The next morning, the sound of the train woke Leonard up.

When he looked around the stars were gone, and so was Marie.

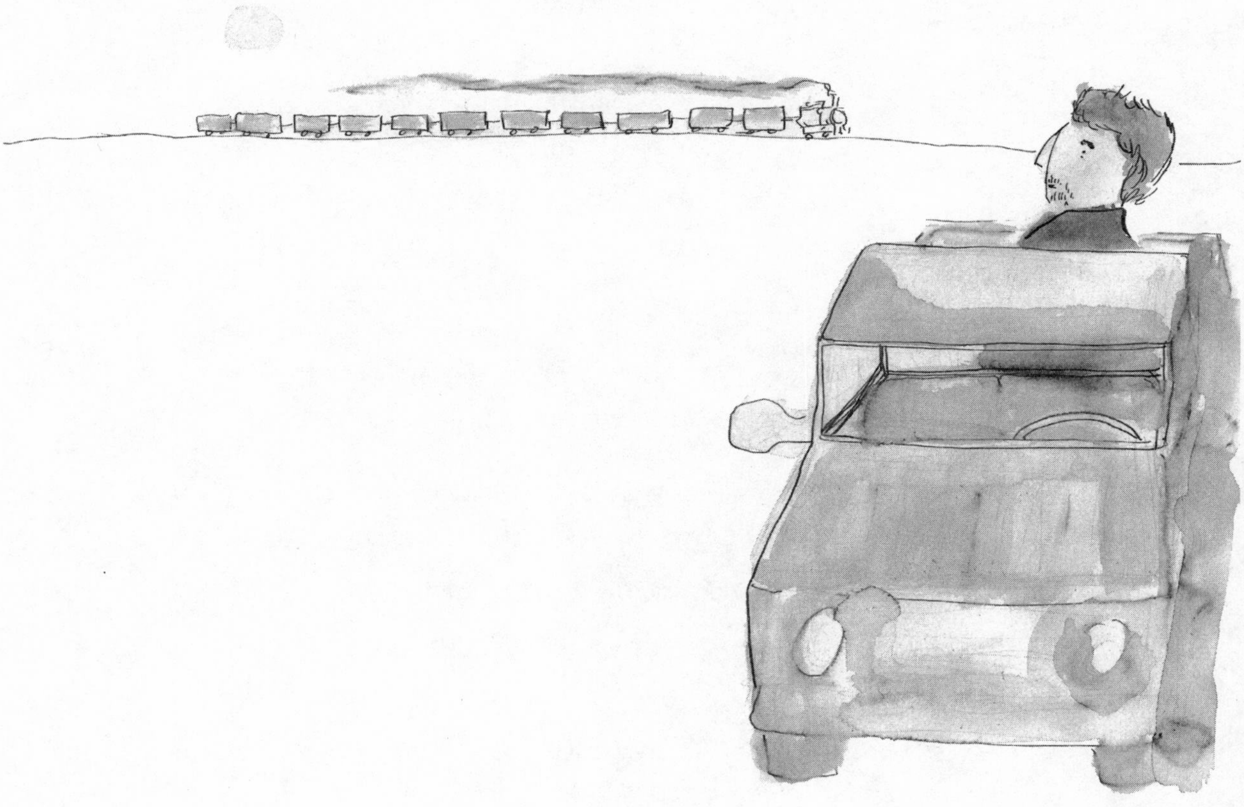

The end.

I killed the wild beast called Anxiety. Don't worry everyone—you're free.

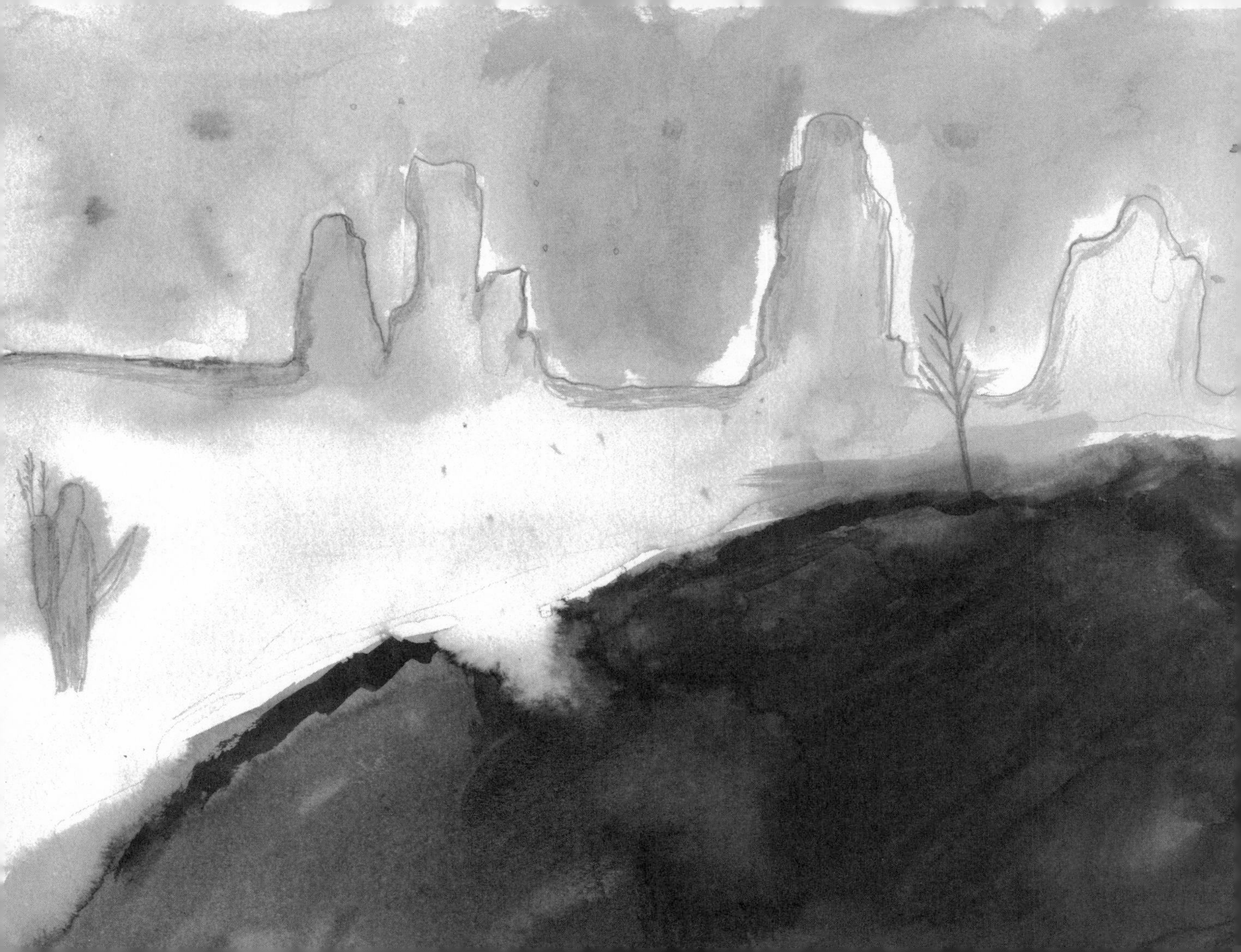

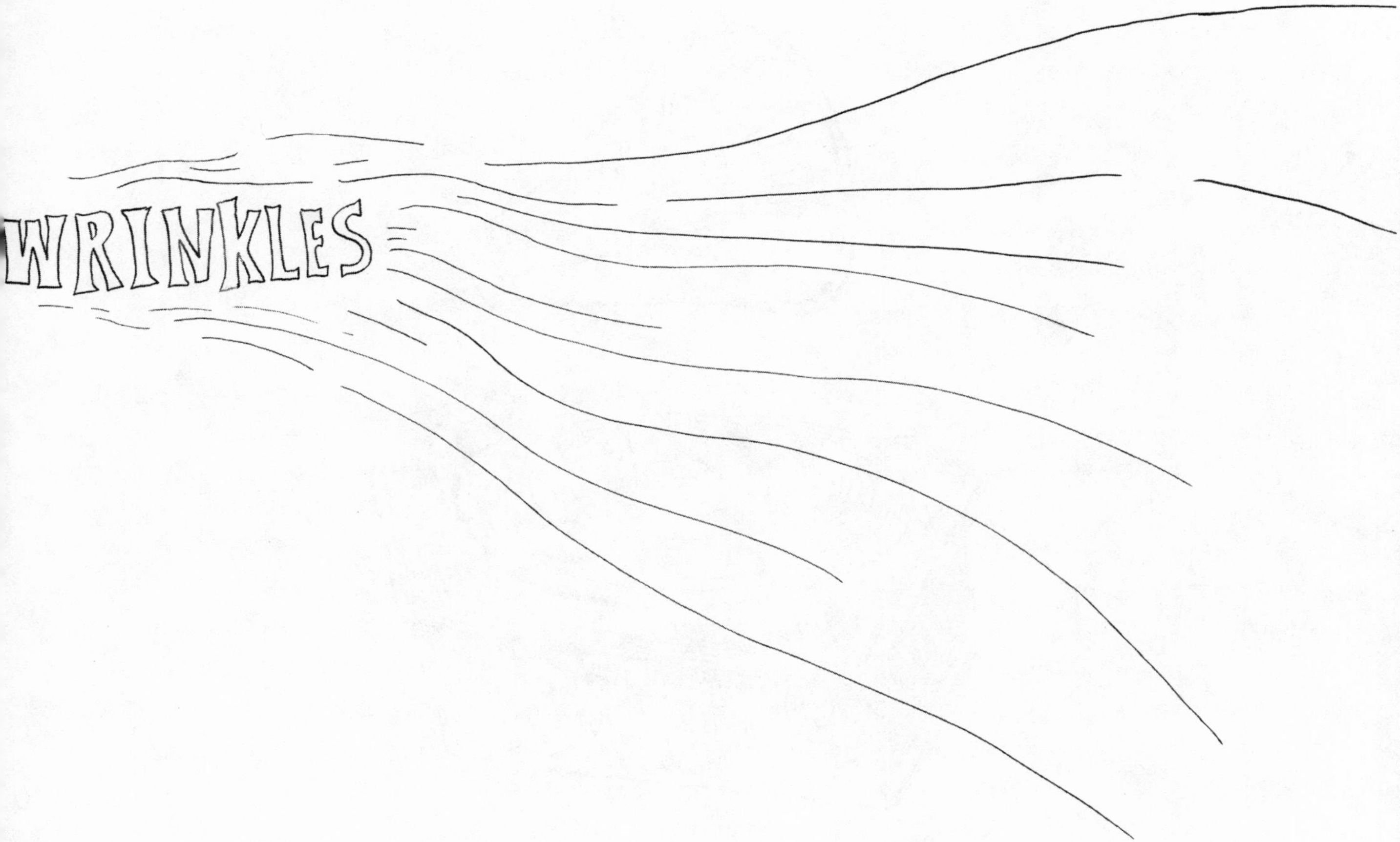
WRINKLES

Our contour lines have been traced by time
for wearing a face for so long, that it is an honor
to have a record embedded on our skin of how
we were known for much of our lives.

This little lady must've smiled a lot.
Even when she is not smiling she is smiling.

This one worried too much
and wore a sexy face from time
to time. Perhaps she was worried
about being TOO sexy . . .

This man was ruled by his sarcasm.
He stressed his skin by punctuating his jokes with
raising his eyebrows and smirking. It is very
difficult to take him seriously even at his most
sincere moments.

If we took a finger and ran it along the grooves that fold around our souls, would it play us a song? Would we hear our heart's soaring melody?

WORDS OF FAREWELL

If you are reading this that means you are alive, your heart is beating right now.

Thank you for existing.

Throughout life you will get hurt, but hold on tight and fight the wild beast of Anxiety. Because it's worth it. Because you're worth it. And you very well might be the thing that can change your own life.

May you never lose romance for the world, and if you do, that's okay. Get out that old ladder and climb on out of your head and back into the world and exist. Because you're important . . . from the day you were born and forever more.

There's so much to live for, give yourself a chance.

Sincerely,

A stranger

Thank you to my handsome-hearted soul mate, Jet, for dreaming with fire and dancing with me endlessly; to my family; Mister Glover for helping me with notes and letting me pay him in eggs; and thank you to you reading this and giving this book life.

About the Author

CHARLYNE YI is a cobbler, fire-eater, comedian, and musician. She can do ten push-ups a day. She wrote and starred in the fictionalized documentary *Paper Heart*, for which she won the Waldo Salt Screenwriting Award at Sundance. She has also been in *Knocked Up*, *This Is 40*, and *House*.